PRETZEL MAKING AT HOME

PRETZEL MAKING
at home

Andrea Slonecker

Photographs by Alex Farnum

CHRONICLE BOOKS

SAN FRANCISCO

Library of Congress Cataloging-in-Publication Data available.
ISBN 978-1-4521-0964-0

Manufactured in China

Designed by Alice Chau
Typesetting by Alice Chau & Helen Lee
Illustrations by Lydia Ortiz
Front cover and author photographs by David Reamer
Prop styling by Christine Wolheim
Food styling by Erin Quon

This book is typeset in Vitesse, Fairplex, DIN, Eames Century Modern, and Fette Fraktur.

Beck's is a registered trademark of Brauerei Beck & Co.
Bitburger is a registered trademark of Bitburger Braugruppe GmbH.
Bob's Red Mill is a registered trademark of Bob's Red Mill Natural Foods Inc.
Formica is a registered trademark of the Diller Corporation.
Microplane is a registered trademark of Grace Manufacturing Inc.
Paulaner is a registered trademark of Paulaner Brauerei GmbH & Co. KG.
Pop Rocks is a registered trademark of Zeta Espacial S.A.
Snyder's of Hanover is a registered trademark of Snyder's-Lance Inc.
Valrhona is a registered trademark of Valrhona S.A.
Warsteiner is a registered trademark of Warsteiner Brauerei Haus Cramer KG.
Weihenstephaner is a registered trademark of Bayerische Staatsbrauerei.
Wondra is a registered trademark of General Mills Inc.

10 9 8 7 6 5 4 3 2 1

Chronicle Books LLC
680 Second Street
San Francisco, California 94107
www.chroniclebooks.com

For my family, including my mentor, Diane Morgan,
who made this big dream of mine possible.

CONTENTS

INTRODUCTION

In Germany and the surrounding region, pretzels symbolize the craft of baking. For centuries, large pretzel-shaped signs made of wood or iron have hung above the doorways of bakeries in this area of Europe. The tradition started in the Middle Ages, when most peasants were illiterate. The distinctive shape of a pretzel was easily recognized, indicating that freshly baked bread was sold inside. The pretzel twist has come to be one of the most iconic food shapes in the world.

In their most basic form, pretzels are made of flour, water, and yeast, which are kneaded together and left to rise. The proofed dough is then lengthened into a rope, looped into a heart-shaped knot, and baked. Most modern recipes include butter, lard, or oil for flavor and tenderness. Sometimes a sweetener is added, sometimes malt, sometimes both. Usually the pretzels are topped with flecks of crunchy salt. However, it is that distinctive pretzel flavor that makes this bread extraordinary, and it's derived from a rather peculiar source: lye.

Years ago when I first visited Germany, I recall hopping a train from Karlsruhe to Munich. Sitting across the aisle, a businessman, suited up and reading the morning paper, pulled out a brown paper bag and began to empty the contents onto the tray in front of him. As the train pulled away from the station, a fat, white sausage and a glistening salted pretzel emerged from the bag. Next the man pulled out a bottle of beer and a glass, a *real* glass, in which he slowly poured the flaxen liquid to a creamy head. It was 8:30 A.M. This was breakfast.

Pretzels are as important to Germans as baguettes are to the French. They are found throughout the country, as well as in neighboring Austria, northern Switzerland, and Alsace, France. In Germany pretzels are most prevalent in the southern state of Bavaria, where they are sold by street vendors, and in cafes and *Biergarten* (beer gardens) at all hours of the day.

When I was a kid, I thought of soft pretzels as an American snack. The ones sold at football stadiums were spongy twisted treats that came with nacho cheese dip; they seemed as all-American to me as the players on the field. The ones I bought from street vendors on trips to big cities came with yellow mustard and were coated with so much acrid salt that I'd have to brush some of it off

A PRETZEL, BY ANY OTHER NAME

It is thought that the Roman Catholic monk who created the first pretzel referred to it as a *pretiola*, or "little reward." But like all pretzel history, there's another possibility. In the Old High German language, the word for "pretzel" was *brezitella*, a term that linguists link to the Latin, *brachiatellum*, which can be loosely translated as "little baked bread with branchlike arms." Another possible Latin root word is *bracchiola*, meaning "little arm," which substantiates the theory that the shape of the pretzel represents a child praying. The German word for "pretzel" now varies with regional dialects—*brezel, bretzel, bretzeln, breze,* and *precia* are all used. In Bavaria, they are known as *brezn, brez'n,* and *brezen.* We can deduce that pretzels were first brought to America in the latter part of the nineteenth century, since the word first appeared in an English-American dictionary in 1879.

before taking a bite. Still, I held soft pretzels in high regard, as a curious treat that I received on rare occasions. As I began researching authentic pretzel recipes for this book, I discovered the cultural significance of this little bread from the land of my German ancestors, and delved into their twisted history.

No scholarly research has provided conclusive evidence on the origins of pretzels. What we do have is more than a millennium's worth of amusing folklore and anecdotal tales. The most common legend about the "invention" of pretzels dates them to the year AD 610, somewhere in the region that is now where northern Italy meets southern France. As the story goes, a monk rolled out scraps of bread dough and fashioned them to resemble a child's arms crossed over his chest in prayer, as was the practice in those days. He baked the little breads and gave them to young parishioners who made an effort to learn Scripture and recite prayers. The breads were called *pretiola*, or "little rewards." In a variation of this story, the pretzels were not bribes for children, but sustenance for fellow monks during the Lenten fast. The shape was to remind them that Lent was a time for prayer and penance. A third plausible theory claims that pretzels were a variation of ring-shaped communion breads, and the shape we know now as a pretzel twist came later, in the twelfth century by some accounts, when pretzels were introduced to the Germanic regions by Roman conquerors.

According to two popular explanations, the flavor we associate with pretzels was an accident. In the first version, a tray of pretzels went from golden and tender to dark and leathery when a baker accidentally dropped them into a potful of lye water, which he would have been using to cure fish and olives and make soup. He baked the pretzels anyway. To his surprise, they emerged from the oven with lacquered, mahogany crusts and a pleasing mineral flavor. Yet another story holds that in 1839 a baker named Anton Nepomuk Pfanenbrenner, working at a cafe in Munich, accidentally brushed his pretzels with a lye-based cleaning solution instead of a sweet glaze. Whichever version is true, pretzels have had their characteristic flavor and shine ever since.

It is believed that German and Swiss-German immigrants brought pretzels to America in the nineteenth century. Many of these immigrants settled in southeastern Pennsylvania, where they were dubbed the Pennsylvania Dutch. (*Deutsche*, the German word for "German," was incorrectly translated as "Dutch.") Italian immigrants in Philadelphia, who were skilled bakers, soon adopted pretzel making and sold the soft pretzels from wood-framed glass boxes on street corners. Pretzels became a popular snack in Pennsylvania. To this day, Pennsylvanians consume twelve times as many pretzels per year as the rest of us.

Hard pretzels were first made in Pennsylvania Dutch Country. According to legend, they were made not for the purpose of preservation, as you might think, but because of another accident. A baker's young apprentice forgot a batch of soft pretzels in the oven one night. The next morning the baker went to light the oven and discovered the petrified pretzels inside. Before throwing out the hardened breads, he tasted one and was delighted by their dense crunch. So he sold them and launched an American snacking phenomenon.

In 1861 the Julius Sturgis Pretzel Bakery opened in Lititz, Pennsylvania, becoming America's first commercial pretzel bakery. In the 1930s, a pretzel-twisting machine was invented that could turn out 245 pretzels per minute, about 200 more than the fastest humans were able to produce. So, in the latter half of the twentieth century, what had been an artisan craft central to German culture became America's favorite factory-produced snack food, available at concession stands and in cellophane bags lining grocery store shelves.

As a result of America's renewed interest in artisan breads, pretzel making has become popular. In New York City's East Village, Lina Kulchinsky operates Sigmund Pretzel Shop, a bakery dedicated to Bavarian-style soft pretzels. At Prime Meats, in Brooklyn, pretzels made in the beautiful Swabian shape—with spindly arms and fat bellies—are served simply with butter, and the leftovers are turned into pretzel dumplings to accompany beef sauerbraten. The German-trained baker Edgar Loesch of Fressen Artisan Bakery in Portland, Oregon, sells authentic pretzels at farmers' markets all over the city. Thanks to the efforts of many bakers and chefs such as these, this country is rediscovering the pleasure of genuine pretzels.

Pretzel Making at Home is dedicated to the craft of handmade pretzels. This cookbook is a tribute to the nearly forgotten methods of making pretzels by hand, which are being resurrected by modern chefs and artisan bakers. No passionate home baker's collection is complete without an understanding of this centuries-old form of baking. Many of these recipes represent traditional German specialties, and others are uniquely American, using the pretzels in innovative ways. There's nothing like the smell of pretzels wafting from your oven, and they're especially satisfying when presented with your own homemade mustard. I include dozens of ideas for shaping, topping, and filling pretzels, and making dips with which to serve them. I invite you to get lost in the pretzel possibilities and come up with your own pretzel logic.

TYING THE KNOT AND OTHER PRETZELISMS

In German-speaking regions of Europe, the twisted pretzel shape is rich with religious symbolism and is a sign of good luck, love, and prosperity. The three vacant holes are said to represent the Holy Trinity: the Father, the Son, and the Holy Spirit. Pretzels are a means of celebrating many holidays, such as Easter, when they are hidden along with eggs, and "Palm pretzels" are made in observance of Palm Sunday. On New Year's Day, they are given to friends and family for good luck in the coming year. Since the Middle Ages, a pretzel's intertwined shape has symbolized the binding contract of marriage, hence the term, "to tie the knot."

PRETZEL BASICS

THE PRETZEL PANTRY

BEER

"Liquid bread" is a key ingredient in most of the pretzel dough recipes in this book. I've experimented with countless combinations of water, milk, and beer, and I'm hands-down sold on the flavor nuances that beer imparts to the pretzel dynamic. Plus, pretzels are native to Germany, so the two belong together. Nearly all of the recipes in this book were developed with pilsner-style beer because I like its full-hop flavor, though a good-quality lager of any type will suffice. (Just stay away from anything you drank out of a can or keg in high school, and you should be fine.) You'll get extra bonus points if you use a German *Pilsener*, such as Bitburger, Warsteiner, or Beck's. In addition to pilsner, two other styles of beer are called for: *Weissbier* and *Doppelbock*. *Weissbier* is Bavarian wheat beer, which is also called *Hefeweizen*. Use any light-colored, cloudy wheat beer—foreign or domestic—in its place. Dark and malty Bavarian *Doppelbock* is a lager-style beer of a different sort. It packs a richer flavor that can stand up to the pungency of mustard seeds in homemade beer mustard. These German brews are available at most specialty markets and beer shops.

BUTTER

I always buy unsalted butter, and you should, too. I want to have control over how much and what type of salt is added to my pretzels, and everything else I make for that matter. Butter is proportionately a small component of a pretzel's ingredients list, but it gives a tremendous amount of flavor and crunch to hard pretzels, and tenderness and moisture to soft ones. It is also why your pretzel crackers will have that tender-crispness; your caramel, that creamy richness; and your pretzel croissant, those defining melt-in-your-mouth, lofty layers.

FLOUR

Most of the structure and flavor of pretzels come from flour. It is the type of flour that you choose and the way that you treat it that will determine the texture of your pretzels. When wheat flour is mixed with water and kneaded, a protein composite called gluten develops. The elastic quality of gluten is tough enough to withstand the pressure of the gases created by yeast during fermentation, allowing the yeasted dough to rise into lofty, chewy pretzels. You will notice that throughout this book, I call for unbleached white flour, which I feel is important. Bleaching flour is an unnecessary alteration that is done for aesthetic reasons. This chemical process produces subtle, metallic off-flavors in your baked goods. Though not traditional, other grain flours, such as rye and spelt, as well as whole-wheat flour, produce complex, malty-caramel flavors and hardy texture in pretzels. Because they have considerably less gluten-forming proteins, they should be used in combination with bread flour to achieve an adequate rise. The fat in whole-grain flours goes rancid relatively quickly, so it is wise to store them in the refrigerator or freezer to lengthen their shelf life by several months. See Resources on page 124.

All-purpose flour As the name implies, all-purpose flour is a middle-of-the-road workhorse in the baker's pantry. If this flour had a tagline it would read, "Jack of all trades, master of none." Yet it has the ability to release enough gluten for airy breads when kneaded, and is mild enough to yield tender pastries when the dough is lightly mixed. For the best results with recipes in this book that call for unbleached all-purpose flour, use a brand with between 10 to 11 percent protein content, such as Gold Medal, which comes in at 10.5 percent.

Bread flour Higher in gluten than all other flours, bread flour is the key to the best quality yeasted breads. I use King Arthur unbleached bread flour, because at 12.7 percent, it has a higher gluten content than other national brands.

Rye flour Dark rye flour produces hearty pretzels with a malty sweetness and a pleasingly coarse texture and density. Light rye flour will impart a subtler flavor and finer texture. I prefer the heftiness of dark rye.

Spelt flour This ancient grain was likely used by the pretzel bakers of antiquity. Mix in whole-grain spelt flour for a distinctly rustic quality in your pretzels, which some find unusual but others rejoice over. There is now the option of refined white spelt flour (sometimes labeled "light"), which you could experiment with as well. For the Spelt Pretzel Dough variation (page 30), I used whole-grain, stone-ground spelt flour from Bob's Red Mill.

Whole-wheat flour The anatomy of a whole grain of wheat includes the outer, fiber-filled bran; the starchy endosperm, which makes up the majority of the volume; and the fat- and nutrient-dense germ. In whole-wheat flour, they are all there. For this reason, whole-wheat flour gives an appealing nuttiness and a granular texture to your pretzels; plus it is more nutritious. I like stone-ground whole-wheat flour.

Gluten-free alternative I seem to have a rapidly increasing number of gluten-free friends, and I wouldn't dare deny them the pleasure of a tasty pretzel. So I tested my soft pretzel dough recipe using a package of Bob's Red Mill Homemade Wonderful GF Bread Mix, and the outcome was a delightful success.

LYE

Food-grade lye (sodium hydroxide, or NaOH) is nothing to fear. It is a naturally occurring alkaline substance that was originally derived from the ashes of hardwood. In addition to pretzels, lye has been used to create such widely consumed foods as cured olives, lutefisk (Scandinavian dried codfish), hominy, and Chinese noodles for hundreds of years. It's also now used to peel mandarin oranges before canning, and it is responsible for that caramel color in soft drinks (and we all know that soft drinks are consumed in vast quantities these days). In this book, I recommend dipping your pretzel dough in a 1 percent lye solution, which is plenty concentrated for a pretzel-y outcome, yet diluted enough to be absolutely safe for consumption once the pretzels are baked. The lye wash breaks down the protein and starch on the surface of the pretzels, so that when they are placed in a hot oven, the gelatinized exterior solidifies into a deep brown, glossy crust. (Chemically, the sodium hydroxide reacts with carbon dioxide in the oven to form edible sodium carbonate.)

Sourcing lye for home use can be done online. I order food-grade lye microbeads in a 2-lb/910-g bottle from Essential Depot (see Resources, page 124). It is enough lye to produce at least sixty batches of pretzels. (You could open a pretzel factory!) Whichever company you source lye from, be sure to read and follow their instructions for safe handling. Dispose of lye by adding a few tablespoons of vinegar to neutralize the pH and then pour it down your sink drain. (This is a bonus as it acts as a homemade drain cleaner.) Store lye in its original container, and always make sure that it is tightly sealed, since it will dissolve simply from moisture in the air. See page 21 for an alternative to lye: baked baking soda.

SALT

No one knows salt better than Mark Bitterman, the owner of The Meadow salt shops in Portland, Oregon, and New York City, and author of the book *Salted: A Manifesto on the World's Most Essential Mineral, with Recipes*. I consulted Mark at his Portland shop one afternoon, determined to find the perfect artisan pretzel salt. Like Mark, I find the flavor of conventional pretzel salt unpleasantly biting and lackluster. In my opinion, salt's role on top of a pretzel is to provide crunch, saltiness, and minerality. The key to a good pretzel salt is in the size and shape of the crystals, plus a nuanced flavor. Rock salts that are mined from the earth are very low in moisture, so they make excellent pretzel salts because they are less likely to dissolve on the surface of the crust. They pack a salty zing and powerful crunch. Salt that is marketed as "pretzel salt" is a low-grade rock salt. Flaky salts are more elegant, with a fleeting salinity and brittle crispness that shatters between your teeth. Bali Rama Pyramid salt is particularly stunning, with a Pop Rocks–style crunch and majestic aesthetic—the crystals resemble the multitiered pyramids of Mesoamerica. In his own recipe for pretzels, Mark uses a Maine hickory-smoked salt for a smoky variation. Flavored artisan salts, such as this one, give you infinite options for pretzel creativity. But go ahead and use conventional pretzel salt if you enjoy its flavor and texture. In the pretzel dough recipes, and all other recipes in this book, I recommend the use of a finely ground sea salt, because I appreciate the flavor of this type of salt more than kosher or (gasp) iodized salts, though kosher salt is an acceptable substitute.

SWEETENERS

Barley malt syrup Thick and dark as molasses, barley malt syrup is half as sweet as table sugar, with a malty, bittersweet taste that will give your pretzels a complex flavor. Look for it in the baking aisle at most specialty markets. In a pinch, substitute an equal amount of dark brown sugar for barley malt syrup in your pretzel dough.

Dark and light brown sugar Both dark and light brown sugars are granulated sugar with molasses added—a little more for dark, a little less for light. Dark brown sugar is the best substitute for barley malt syrup in pretzel dough, because it has a deeper molasses flavor. In general, the two brown sugars can be used interchangeably in most recipes, with little difference.

Granulated sugar Refined white sugar crystals give the perfect texture and sweetness to cinnamon-sugar and boil into rich, golden caramel—one of your pretzels' greatest allies.

Honey The flavor of honey varies widely, depending on the type of flowers from which the bees collect their pollen. For honeyed pretzels, use mild-flavored orange blossom or clover honey, but choose one that is of good quality because you will indeed be able to taste the difference.

YEAST

Yeast is alive. And like any living thing, it is subject to aging and can be a little finicky, so it should be handled with care. Yeast begins to die when it is exposed to temperatures above 120°F/48°C, so be sure to "bloom" yeast in liquids that range between 100 and 115°F/38 and 45°C. During this activation stage, the yeast should become foamy within 5 to 7 minutes. If it doesn't, it is probably dead, so discard it and start over with fresh yeast. The recipes in this book call for active dry yeast, which is typically sold in a strip of three ¼-oz/7-g packets, which equal 2¼ tsp of yeast granules in each one. If you plan to do a lot of pretzel baking, seek out a 4-oz/115-g jar, which is equal to 16 packets and is always more cost-effective. Store yeast in the refrigerator to extend its shelf life.

TOOLS FOR THE PRETZEL BAKER

BAKING SHEETS

Baking sheets, or sheet pans as they are known in a professional kitchen, are usually made of aluminum or stainless steel and can be rimmed, rimless, or partially rimmed for sliding cookies onto a cooling rack (these are called cookie sheets). I prefer to use rimmed aluminum baking sheets that are 12 by 17 in/30.5 by 43 cm. For anything you bake that has a tendency to melt, ooze, or seep, such as croissants, or anything that needs to be contained, like croutons, be sure that your baking sheets are rimmed to avoid a messy oven floor. Always buy baking sheets that are light colored to promote even cooking. Darker baking sheets tend to over-brown the bottoms of your pretzels and cookies.

BENCH SCRAPER

Doubling as both a dough cutter and a cleaning tool for scraping leftover flour off your work surface, a bench scraper, or bench knife, has a large, rectangular stainless-steel blade (or sometimes hard plastic) that is relatively dull, but sharp enough to portion dough beautifully.

HANDS

No piece of equipment is more important for creating perfect pretzels than your own hands. You need them to learn the feel of the dough, roll out long ropes, and twist them into shapes. The more you touch the dough with your hands, the better you will get to know it, and the finer your pretzels will be.

HEAT-PROOF SILICONE SPATULA

I reach for a heat-proof silicone spatula for nearly all of my mixing and stirring needs. The flat tip provides the most surface area for stirring the bottom of a pot, and it allows you to remove every last speck of custard or sauce from the pan. I use Le Creuset brand silicone spatulas, which are heat-resistant up to 482°F/250°C. I don't even own spatulas that aren't heat-proof; there's no need.

OVEN THERMOMETER

Oven temperatures in most home kitchens are off by as much as 50°F/10°C in either direction—too hot or too cold. If you don't have your oven calibrated on occasion, invest in an inexpensive oven thermometer and check to see whether your oven is off and by how much. Adjust your oven temperature as needed before baking.

PARCHMENT PAPER

I use parchment paper for all my baking. It is a surefire way to prevent food from sticking to the pan, and even more important, it makes cleanup easier. Some days I bake several batches of pretzels, and it's so nice to not have to wash the baking sheets after each round. I buy precut, unbleached parchment paper sheets, which fit standard baking sheets perfectly. The manufacturer says they are heat-resistant up to 428°F/220°C, but I find that they work just fine for baking pretzels at 500°F/260°C. Though the paper does turn brown and a little brittle around the edges, this does not affect the flavor. If this worries you, King Arthur Flour sells parchment paper that is heat-resistant up to 500°F/260°C for a single use. If you have nonstick silicone baking mats, such as Silpats, use these instead of parchment paper. The thinner ones work best.

POTS AND PANS FOR PRETZEL DIPPING

For dipping your pretzels in the alkaline solution, it is important to select a vessel that is at least a finger's length greater in diameter than the width of the pretzels and tall enough so that the water comes up no more than 2 in/5 cm from the rim.

This is because you will be turning the pretzels in the hot solution, and the liquid may splash out if the pot is not big enough. Stainless-steel pots are the best choice; be sure to avoid other metal surfaces, such as aluminum, copper, and cast-iron, which will react with the lye, as well as nonstick. I use a flat-bottom, stainless-steel stove-top wok for easier pretzel maneuvering. For pretzel sticks, I use a large stainless-steel roasting pan to accommodate their length.

PROTECTIVE EYEWEAR

A splash or any residual steam from the alkaline pretzel dip will irritate your eyes. To prevent this, you can sport protective eyewear, such as swimming goggles or onion goggles, which are available at cooking supply stores.

RUBBER GLOVES

When adding lye to warm water for dipping pretzels, rubber household gloves—like those lovely bright yellow ones—are a must. The gloves should cover your forearms to prevent irritation in the event that you splash the lye mixture. If you get a pair that fit snuggly and are lined with cotton or foam, do as the professional pretzel bakers do and use your gloved hands to dip the pretzels in the hot lye solution. I find this to be the most efficient method of dipping, but note that this does not work for the Baked Baking Soda Method (see page 21), since the solution is actually simmering on the stove so it is far too hot to touch, even with gloves on.

SKIMMER

A large stainless-steel skimmer is an indispensible component of the pretzel maker's tool kit. Use it to pluck pretzels from their alkaline bath. I'm partial to an Asian-style skimmer, known as a spider, which has a huge shallow basket and an exceptionally wide wire-mesh design for speedy draining.

SPRAY BOTTLE

An all-purpose plastic spray bottle with an adjustable nozzle makes it easy to mist your work surface if you need more friction while shaping pretzels. You'll need an extra spray bottle for making Buttery Pretzel Crackers (page 83).

STAND MIXER

A good, sturdy stand mixer is a lifetime investment. I'm partial to the KitchenAid professional mixers for kneading dense pretzel dough. If you have the classic model, or another brand of stand mixer, note that the dough hook and bowl attachments tend to be flimsier, so you should monitor the kneading process to be sure they don't detach. If you don't have a stand mixer, or you just prefer to knead pretzel dough by hand, that's great because you'll get a better feel for your dough.

WORK SURFACE

Your work surface—a kitchen countertop I presume—is an important piece of "equipment" for pretzel shaping. Many of the recipes in this book require a fair amount of flat work space for tasks such as rolling out long dough ropes. For a large slab of croissant dough or buttery crackers, this surface must be a cold one, to prevent the butter from softening. Wood surfaces are especially nice for handling bread dough because their porousness creates good friction for shaping. Smooth granite countertops, which maintain a cool temperature, are also ideal; that's what I have and I love the way it handles dough. Stainless steel and Formica work just fine as well. If necessary, spray your work surface with water for more friction. Flour has the opposite effect, so try to avoid dusting your work surface unless the dough is too sticky.

TECHNIQUES FOR PRETZEL MAKING

TIMING

Pretzel making is a satisfying baking project to undertake on a weekend afternoon, but don't forget to start your dough the night before for the best-flavored pretzels. Pretzel dough develops a yeasty, sourdoughlike tang when placed in the refrigerator to slowly ferment overnight. Bakers call this retarding the dough. Sometimes I let the dough retard for as long as 36 hours, but that's about the maximum time you should let it go, or the dough will become sticky and mushy. If you want to bake same-day pretzels, follow the instructions for the quick-rise method in the master recipe (see page 26). But I highly recommend waiting out the slow rise, as the pretzels are remarkably more flavorful. Traditional mustard recipes take time as well (at least three weeks, in my opinion) to reach the point where the stinging pungency of ground mustard seeds has mellowed to a complex, palatable heat. In this book I've also offered a few recipes for "instant" mustards for you to enjoy with your fresh pretzels on a whim. Still, for many of the recipes in this book, patience is not a virtue; it is a necessity.

MEASURING FLOUR

Use the "spoon and sweep" method for measuring flour. This means that you are spooning the flour from a flour sack or bin into a measuring cup and sweeping the top with a straightedge to level it off. If you dip your measuring cup into the flour, scoop it up, and then sweep, the flour will be compacted and you will get a radically different measurement, as much as a quarter more flour. A weight measure is always the most accurate, so if you have a kitchen scale, use the gram measurement listed in the recipe.

SHAPING PRETZELS

Pretzels are one of the most recognizable foods in the world because of their ingenious twisted design. This classic shape is created by lengthening a hunk of dough into a rope, and then lassoing it in the air so it tumbles down into a heart-shaped twist. It takes a little practice to become an expert pretzel twister, so don't expect that you will master the shaping technique on your first try. Start by shaping the dough on the work surface as described in the master recipe for soft pretzels (see page 26), rather than in the air, until you get the hang of it. In this book, I refer to the ends of the dough rope as the pretzel's "arms" and the center of the rope as the "belly." I think that a classically shaped pretzel should offer two distinctly different eating experiences: thin, crunchy arms and fat, chewy bellies. In Germany, breads of various shapes are created in the pretzel style—that is, they are dipped in lye solution before baking. These pretzel-flavored breads are not called pretzels, but *laugengebäck*, or "lye pastries." But I still refer to them as pretzels because of their unmistakable flavor and their crusts' pretzel-y appearance. See page 31 for a variety of shaping ideas.

When pretzel dough is pulled from overnight refrigeration, it is quite firm. I find that stiffness actually makes the dough easier to work with. When the dough is warm, it continues to ferment, producing gas bubbles in the dough. If you are working in a warm kitchen on a hot day, this will be an issue. Try to gently twist the dough ropes, pushing the air bubbles out through the ends. You can also refrigerate or freeze a chunk of dough briefly before shaping it to make it more manageable. Save pretzel making for another time if it is a hot day and you have no air-conditioning.

DIPPING PRETZELS IN AN ALKALINE SOLUTION

Dipping pretzels in a solution of a small amount of food-grade lye dissolved in water gives them that unique pretzel flavor. Unfortunately, food-grade lye is unavailable in most retail stores, making it difficult to source and use for home cooks. That's why most recipes for homemade pretzels substitute baking soda (which is much less alkaline), but the pretzel flavor and the quality of the crust are substandard with this method. In 2010 the esteemed food scientist Harold McGee wrote a story for the *New York Times* in which he explained that the chemical properties of baking soda can be altered, causing it to behave in a similar way to lye, if it is baked in an oven at a low temperature for an hour or so. I have found this to be true. Still, there is no replicating that genuine pretzel-y quality that a lye dip imparts, so in this book both options are offered. I prefer the lye method and always have lye on hand, but I also thoroughly enjoy pretzels made with a baked baking soda substitute. See following for instructions. For information on where to buy food-grade lye, see Resources, page 124.

Lye method Before you begin working with lye, there are a few precautions to take, since it is a hazardous chemical when it's not handled properly. Always wear rubber household gloves that cover your forearms, as it will irritate your skin. Be extremely careful not to let lye water splash on you, and avoid touching the dipped pretzels with bare hands until after they are baked. Also, consider wearing protective eyewear (see page 18). Make the solution in a well-ventilated room, have the stove's hood vent on high power, and avoid hovering directly over the pot if there is any residual steam. Protective eyewear will also shield your eyes from steam that may irritate them when you open the oven door while the pretzels are baking. Or you can simply open the door and let the steam escape before leaning in, which is what I do. While all this sounds a little dangerous for a home kitchen, I've found that with these simple precautions, dipping pretzels in a lye solution is a safe and worthwhile endeavor that makes a huge difference in the authenticity of your pretzels.

To get a crust with a deeply browned, lacquered appearance, the lye must be hot when the pretzels are dipped. You can prepare a cool lye bath by dissolving the lye in lukewarm water straight from the tap, without heating it, but the pretzels will emerge from the oven with a lighter caramel hue.

To make the lye solution for soft pretzels: Select a large stainless-steel pot at least a finger's length greater in diameter than the width of the pretzels and tall enough so that the water comes up no more than 2 in/5 cm from the rim. (For more information on choosing a pot, see page 16.) Fill the pot with 6 cups/1.4 L of water. Wearing rubber gloves, add the lye, 1 tbsp at a time. With the hood vent on, warm the lye solution over high heat just until you see wisps of steam, and then remove the pot from the heat and cool the water until the steam subsides, about 5 minutes.

Baked baking soda method An alternative to working with lye is to dip pretzels in a simmering baked baking soda solution, which will give you a result that is close to the dark, burnished crust that lye imparts. If you prefer to avoid working with lye, or just don't have time to source it, use this method.

To make the baked baking soda solution: First, you must bake the baking soda. This step should be done while the pretzels are undergoing their first rise, if not earlier. Preheat the oven to 250°F/120°C/gas ½. For one batch of pretzels, spread out ¼ cup/70 g of baking soda on an aluminum pie pan or a small rimmed baking sheet covered with aluminum foil. Bake the baking soda for 1 hour. The baking soda will lose weight as it bakes but maintains about the same volume, so you should end up with about ¼ cup/60 g of baked baking soda. Allow it to cool completely, and then keep it in an airtight container at room temperature until you are ready to make pretzels. (If you see more than one batch of pretzels in your future, consider baking a whole box of baking soda in one shot, since it keeps indefinitely. Sift baked baking soda before using, as it cakes after prolonged storage.) Select a large stainless-steel pot and fill it with 8 cups/2 L of water. Be sure to choose a pot that is at least a finger's length wider than the diameter of the pretzels and tall enough so that the water comes up no more than 2 in/5 cm from the rim. (Avoid other metal surfaces, such as aluminum and copper, and nonstick surfaces, which may react with the baked baking soda.) Pour in the ¼ cup/60 g of baked baking soda, and bring the liquid to a simmer over medium-high heat. Once the baking soda dissolves, reduce the heat to medium to maintain a gentle simmer. Before baking, brush the tops of the pretzels lightly with an egg wash of 1 egg yolk, beaten with 1 tbsp of water. This will give them a glossy finish.

SCORING

For soft pretzels, make a slash in the pretzel dough to control where the dough will split as steam escapes while they bake. This will avoid ragged cracks in your finished pretzels. Use a sharp paring knife, or better yet, a razor blade, to make a deep slit in the thickest part of each pretzel. This is only necessary for the classic pretzel shape and pretzel rolls, but it can be done on pretzel bites and sticks, if you like.

BAKING

A very hot oven temperature of 500°F/260°C/gas 10 is necessary to achieve that deep mahogany color characteristic of artisan soft pretzels. Hard pretzels have no trouble reaching the desired darkness by the time they are crisped on the inside, so they bake at a much lower temperature. In fact, be careful not to burn them by monitoring their progress as they near the end of the baking time.

STORING

Soft pretzels Soft pretzels keep at room temperature, without being wrapped up or enclosed in a container, for about 12 hours. If you plan to enjoy at least some of them later, don't salt them before baking. Just salt the ones you plan to eat the same day. When soft pretzels are stored in an airtight container or are wrapped in plastic—a necessity to keep them from drying out—the trapped humidity will dissolve the salt crystals on the surface of the crust. You'll end up with droplets of water and swollen, soggy spots where the salt once was. Store your soft pretzels in an airtight container or wrap each one tightly in plastic wrap, and keep them at room temperature (or in the refrigerator if they have a cheesy or meaty filling or topping) for up to 2 days. Or place the pretzels, tightly wrapped in plastic, in a resealable plastic freezer bag, and freeze for up to 1 month. Reheat room-temperature pretzels in a 350°F/180°C/ gas 4 oven for about 5 minutes. Or, without defrosting, reheat frozen pretzels until they are warmed through, 10 to 12 minutes. When you are ready to eat them, brush the unsalted crusts lightly with melted butter and sprinkle on the coarse salt.

Hard pretzels Store hard pretzels at room temperature in an airtight container. They will keep for about 2 weeks.

SOFT PRETZELS

The first recipe in this chapter is for classic soft pretzels, which functions as a master recipe for the entire chapter. For your first pretzel-making experience, I highly recommend that you start with this traditional recipe. There is nothing more satisfying than pulling your very first batch of glistening soft pretzels out of the oven and eating one, simply spread with cold butter, which melts from the heat of the warm bread. Then experiment with different doughs, pretzel shapes, and toppings to achieve entirely different flavors and textures in your pretzels. Use the recipes that follow to produce other sweet and savory pretzel creations. In the second half of the chapter, you'll discover ideas for serving pretzels as sandwiches, dumplings, bread pudding, and stuffing.

One ¼-oz/7-g package active dry yeast (2¼ tsp)

½ cup/120 ml warm water (between 100 and 115°F/38 and 45°C)

1 tbsp barley malt syrup (see page 15) or 1 tbsp firmly packed dark brown sugar

3¼ cups/420 g unbleached bread flour

½ cup/120 ml cold pilsner-style beer

2 tbsp unsalted butter, cubed, at room temperature, plus more for greasing the bowl

2 tsp fine sea salt, such as *fleur de sel* or *sel gris*

2 tbsp food-grade lye (see page 20), or ¼ cup/ 60 g baked baking soda (see page 21)

Topping (optional; see page 35 for Topping Options)

makes 8

TRADITIONAL SOFT PRETZELS (MASTER RECIPE)

If you've ever tasted a real German soft pretzel, with a deep, dark, burnished skin showered with crunchy salt crystals, and a yeasty, chewy middle, then you know what you're in for here. The shape of these pretzels is typical of the historic German cultural region known as Swabia, where the tradition is to shape pretzels with fat "bellies" and thinly tapered, crispy "arms" interlocking in a twisted embrace. The bellies are slashed with a long, deep slit in the bottom to allow steam to escape as they bake. To prepare the best pretzels, you'll need to begin a day, or at least 8 hours, in advance and let the dough slowly rise in the refrigerator. While an option for making quick pretzels is given, too, I highly recommend the overnight method because the dough's flavor really develops during the slow fermentation, becoming nuanced with a yeasty tang that is worth every moment of anticipation. A dip in a solution of food-grade lye and water before baking sets pretzels apart from other yeasted breads. If you aren't up to the challenge of sourcing and working with lye, I've offered a suitable alternative: baked baking soda (see page 21). The pages that follow this master recipe are filled with dough variations, alternative shapes, and topping options.

MIXING AND PROOFING

Sprinkle the yeast over the warm water in the bowl of a stand mixer or in a large bowl. Add the barley malt syrup, stirring until it is dissolved. Allow the yeast to bloom until it is foamy, 5 to 7 minutes. Stir in the flour, beer, butter, and salt and continue stirring to form a shaggy mass. Attach the bowl and the dough hook to the stand mixer and begin kneading on medium-low speed. After about 1 minute the dough will form a smooth ball. The dough should be quite firm and may be slightly tacky, but not sticky. (If it is sticky, add a little more flour, about 1 tbsp at a time, and knead it in until the dough is smooth. If the dough is too dry to come together, add more water, 1 tsp at a time.) Continue kneading the dough on medium-low speed until it is elastic, 5 to 7 minutes. Alternatively, turn the shaggy dough out onto an unfloured work surface and knead it by hand.

Choose a bowl that will be large enough to contain the dough after it has doubled in size, and grease it lightly with butter. Transfer the dough to the greased bowl and cover the bowl tightly with plastic wrap. Put the dough in the refrigerator to rise for at least 8 hours, and up to 24 hours, for optimal flavor.

For quick pretzels, allow the dough to rise at room temperature (in a warm spot) until it has doubled in size, about 1½ hours.

SHAPING
Line two 12-by-17-in/30.5-by-43-cm rimmed baking sheets with parchment paper; set aside.

Turn the dough out onto an unfloured work surface and firmly press it down to deflate. To form the classic pretzel shape, cut the dough into eight equal portions. Work with one piece of dough at a time and keep the rest covered with a damp, clean kitchen towel. Pat a piece of dough down with your fingertips to form a rough rectangle about 3½ by 5½ in/9 by 14 cm. Beginning on a long side, roll the dough up tightly, forming it into a little loaf. Pinch the seam together. Shape the dough into a rope by rolling it against the work surface with your palms and applying mild pressure, working from the center of the dough out to the ends. If you need more friction, spray the counter with a little water from a squirt bottle or drizzle a few drops of water and spread it with your hand. Once you can feel that the dough rope doesn't want to stretch any farther (usually when it is between 12 to 16 in/30.5 to 40.5 cm long), set it aside to rest and begin shaping another piece in the same manner. Repeat this process with the remaining pieces of dough.

continued

Return to the first dough rope and continue rolling it out to a length of 24 to 28 in/61 to 71 cm, leaving the center about 1 in/2.5 cm in diameter and tapering the ends thinly by applying a little more pressure as you work your way out. Position the dough rope into a U shape, with the ends pointing away from you. Holding an end in each hand, cross the ends about 3 in/7.5 cm from the tips and then cross them again. Fold the ends down and press them into the U at about 4 and 8 o'clock, allowing about ¼ in/6 mm of the ends to over-hang. Place the pretzel on one of the prepared baking sheets and cover it with a damp towel. Repeat this process with the remaining dough, spacing out the pretzels on the baking sheets at least 1 in/2.5 cm apart and covering them with a damp towel.

Allow the covered pretzels to rise at warm room temperature until they have increased in size by about half, 20 to 30 minutes. (The pretzels can be refrigerated at this point, covered tightly with plastic wrap, for up to 8 hours before dipping and baking them.)

At least 20 minutes before baking, position one rack in the upper third and another rack in the lower third of the oven and preheat it to 500°F/260°C/gas 10.

DIPPING

Use the lye solution (see page 20) or baked baking soda solution (see page 21).

Use a large skimmer to gently dip the pretzels in the lye or baked baking soda solution, one or two at a time. Leave them in the solution for about 20 seconds, carefully turning once after 10 seconds. Remove the pretzels from the liquid, drain, and return them to the baking sheets, spacing them at least 1 in/2.5 cm apart. If the ends come detached, simply reposition them. Repeat with the remaining pretzels.

TOPPING AND BAKING

Use a sharp paring knife or razor blade to cut a slit about ¼ in/6 mm deep in the thickest part of each pretzel (the bottom of the U). Top them as you choose, if desired.

Bake the pretzels until they are deep mahogany in color, 8 to 12 minutes, rotating the pans from front to back and top to bottom halfway through the baking time. Transfer the pretzels to a rack to cool for 10 minutes before serving. The pretzels are best enjoyed the day they are made, ideally warm from the oven or within an hour of being baked.

STORING

To store the pretzels, allow them to cool completely and then wrap each one individually in plastic wrap. Store them at room temperature for up to 2 days, or put the plastic-wrapped pretzels in a resealable plastic freezer bag and freeze them for up to 1 month. Reheat the pretzels in a 350°F/180°C/gas 4 oven for about 5 minutes, or for 10 to 12 minutes if frozen.

COOK'S NOTE:

To prepare a half batch of the dough, use the following ingredient quantities: 1½ tsp active dry yeast; ¼ cup/60 ml warm water (between 100 and 115°F/38 and 45°C); 1½ tsp barley malt syrup or 1½ tsp firmly packed dark brown sugar; 1½ cups plus 2 tbsp/210 g unbleached bread flour; ¼ cup/60 ml cold pilsner-style beer; 1 tbsp unsalted butter, cubed, at room temperature, plus more for greasing the bowl; 1 tsp fine sea salt, such as *fleur de sel* or *sel gris.*

DOUGH VARIATIONS

WHOLE-WHEAT PRETZEL DOUGH

Substitute 1¼ cups/155 g of whole-wheat flour for 1¼ cups/160 g of the bread flour.

SPELT PRETZEL DOUGH

Substitute 1¼ cups/155 g of whole-grain spelt flour for 1¼ cups/160 g of the bread flour.

CARAWAY-RYE PRETZEL DOUGH

Substitute 1¼ cups/155 g of dark rye flour for 1¼ cups/160 g of the bread flour. Add 1½ tbsp of toasted caraway seeds to the dough mixture before kneading. Top the pretzels with more toasted caraway seeds before baking.

OLIVE AND GARLIC PRETZEL DOUGH

Reduce the quantity of beer to ⅓ cup/75 ml. Add ½ cup/100 g of well-drained, pitted, and roughly chopped kalamata olives; 1 tbsp of minced garlic; and 1 tbsp of chopped fresh thyme to the dough mixture before kneading. This variation is especially good topped with crumbled feta cheese (see page 35).

CINNAMON-RAISIN PRETZEL DOUGH

Increase the quantity of warm water to 1 cup plus 1 tbsp/255 ml and eliminate the beer. Instead of barley malt syrup, use 3 tbsp of firmly packed dark brown sugar. Reduce the salt to ½ tsp. Add ½ cup/85 g of raisins and 3 tbsp of ground cinnamon to the dough mixture before kneading. When shaping, some of the raisins may fly out of the dough; simply push them back in, or just don't worry about losing a few. A topping of Cinnamon-Sugar (page 35) makes these exceptionally delicious. Serve them smeared with Whipped Cream Cheese with Lemon and Vanilla (page 120) or drizzled with Vanilla Icing (see page 35).

GLUTEN-FREE PRETZEL DOUGH

Substitute one 1-lb/455-g package of Bob's Red Mill Homemade Wonderful GF Bread Mix (see Resources, page 124) for the bread flour. Decrease the quantity of warm water to ¼ cup/60 ml, and replace the yeast with the packet that comes with the mix. Instead of barley malt syrup, add 2 tbsp of firmly packed dark brown sugar to the yeast mixture. Replace the pilsner with a light gluten-free ale (such as New Planet Tread Lightly Ale), and reduce the quantity to ¼ cup/60 ml. Add 2 egg whites, 1 large beaten egg, and 1 tsp apple cider vinegar to the yeast mixture along with the bread mix, beer, butter, and salt. Knead the dough in the stand mixer until it forms a homogenous mass, 3 to 4 minutes, scraping down the sides of the bowl as needed. Form it into a smooth ball with your hands, and proceed with the recipe as instructed. Brush the pretzels lightly with an egg wash of 1 egg yolk beaten with 1 tbsp of water before topping and baking.

SHAPES

NEW YORK STYLE

Pretzels sold by New York City street vendors are larger. The arms are not tapered to thin strands of dough like pretzels in the traditional Swabian shape, but rather are kept plump. To achieve this, follow the instructions for shaping the pretzels in the master recipe, making the following changes: Divide the dough into six equal portions. Shape each portion of dough into a 36-in/91-cm rope, applying even pressure as you roll from the center of the dough to the ends to avoid tapering them. Proceed as instructed in the recipe. ***Makes 6.***

PHILADELPHIA STYLE

In Philadelphia, soft pretzels are oblong, as if the classic pretzel shape was squashed into an infinity sign. These compressed pretzels are baked together, connected like a chain, so that they come out of the oven ready to be pulled apart. To achieve this, follow the instructions for shaping the pretzels, making the following changes: Shape each portion

into a 26-in/66-cm rope, applying even pressure as you roll from the center of the dough to the ends to avoid tapering them. Shape the pretzel into the classic pretzel shape, but attach the ends of the rope to the U at 3 and 9 o'clock. Pull the sides of each pretzel out to elongate the pretzel into an oval shape resembling an infinity sign. Let them rise, and then proceed with dipping as instructed in the recipe. Arrange a chain of four pretzels on each baking sheet so that they are touching. There is no need to slit the dough before baking. Proceed as instructed in the recipe. ***Makes 8.***

ÜBERS

During Oktoberfest, Bavarian *Biergarten* peddle giant pretzels. To make them at home, you'll need plenty of counter space to shape the dough. Follow the instructions for shaping the pretzels, making the following changes: Divide the dough into four equal portions. Shape each one into a 45-in/114-cm rope, applying even pressure as you roll from the center of the dough to the ends; the arms of the pretzels should be just slightly tapered. Proceed as instructed in the recipe, but reduce the oven temperature to 450°F/230°C/gas 8 and increase the baking time to 11 to 15 minutes. ***Makes 4.***

MINIS

Three-bite soft pretzel minis are ideal party fare. Follow the instructions for shaping the pretzels, making the following changes: Divide the dough into twenty-four equal portions. Shape each one into an 18-in/46-cm rope, applying even pressure as you roll from the center of the dough to the ends; the arms of the pretzels should be just slightly tapered. Proceed with shaping as instructed in the recipe. When the first baking sheet is filled with 12 pretzels, cover them with a damp towel and transfer to the refrigerator while you shape the rest of the pretzels to prevent the first batch from overproofing. When all the pretzels are shaped, remove the baking sheet from the refrigerator, and leave all the pretzels at room temperature, covered with damp towels, for the second rise. Since they're small, dip these pretzels in batches of three to five at a time. Decrease the baking time to 8 to 10 minutes. *Makes 24.*

BITES

These are the perfect snack when you're watching a movie. To create bite-size pretzels, make the following changes: Reduce the ingredients to make a half batch of the dough (see Cook's Note, page 29). Divide the dough into eight equal portions. Shape each portion of dough into a 12-in/30.5-cm rope, applying even pressure as you roll from the center of the dough to the ends to avoid tapering them.

Cut the ropes into 1-in/2.5-cm pieces. Proceed as instructed in the recipe, but dip the pretzel bites in batches of at least eight to ten (or more if your pot is large enough). Reduce the baking time to 6 to 9 minutes. *Makes 8 dozen.*

STICKS

Pretzel sticks are the easiest shape to create. The dough is simply rolled out into slender, flute-shaped batons with no twisting required. Follow the instructions for shaping the pretzels, making the following changes: Divide the dough into twenty-four equal portions. Shape each piece of dough into a 12-in/30.5-cm stick, applying even pressure as you roll from the center of the dough to the ends. Apply more pressure at the ends to dramatically taper them to fine points. Note that you'll need to prepare the dipping solution in a pot or pan that is wide enough to accommodate the sticks, such as a stainless-steel roasting pan. If you'd like, use a sharp paring knife or razor blade to make three to five deep, diagonal slashes in the dough before baking. Proceed as instructed in the recipe, decreasing the baking time to 7 to 10 minutes. *Makes 24.*

KNOTS

Pretzel knots are great for topping with cheese or streusel. Follow the instructions for shaping the pretzels, making the following changes: Divide the dough into twelve equal portions. Shape each piece of dough into a 12-in/30.5-cm rope, tapering the ends slightly as you roll from the center of the dough to the ends. Loop the dough into a loose knot without tugging or stretching. There is no need to slash the dough before baking. Proceed as instructed in the recipe. ***Makes 12.***

ROLLS

Pretzel dough can be fashioned into dinner rolls for a dazzling addition to your breadbasket or a clever bun for sliders. Follow the instructions for shaping the pretzels, making the following changes: Divide the dough into twelve equal portions. Working with one portion at a time, pat the dough down with your fingertips to form a 4-in/10-cm circle. Lightly dust the work surface and dough with flour if it is sticky. Fold over the edges of the circle so that they meet

in the middle. Pinch the seams together and turn the roll over so that the seam-side is down. Cup your hand over the dough ball and roll it rapidly against the work surface to smooth out the seams and create a well-shaped sphere. Repeat this process with the remaining dough. Use a sharp paring knife or a razor blade to slit a large, deep cross into the top of each roll before baking. Proceed as instructed in the recipe. ***Makes 12.***

TORPEDO ROLLS

Shaped like little footballs, torpedo rolls have fat middles with pointy ends. This is the most loaflike pretzel shape, so it is a great choice for hoagie or submarine rolls, or sausage buns. To form the torpedo shape, follow the instructions for shaping the pretzels, making the following changes: Divide the dough into six equal portions. Roll up each portion into a little loaf and roll the loaf against the counter with your palms at an angle to taper the ends to a fine point. Try not to elongate the loaf to more than 8 in/20 cm. Use a sharp paring knife or razor blade to make three diagonal slashes ¼ in/6 mm deep before baking. Proceed as instructed in the recipe. ***Makes 6.***

TWISTS

This twisted pretzel roll is my favorite shape, inspired by the ones at Grüner restaurant in Portland, Oregon. Shaping them takes a little more practice than most of the other styles. Begin by following the instructions for shaping the pretzels, making the following changes: Divide the dough into six equal portions. Shape each portion into a 36-in/91-cm rope, applying even pressure as you roll from the center of the dough to the ends to avoid tapering them. Working with one rope at a time, grab both ends and hold it up in the air in a U shape. Briskly lasso one side of the U around the other, intertwining the dough in a twist. When the twisting loses its momentum, put a finger in the loop that forms at the bottom of the U and continue to twist it manually, as the bottom half of the dough naturally curls up, and the bottom loop meets the ends. Insert the ends through the loop to secure the twist. There is no need to slash the dough before baking. Proceed as instructed in the recipe. ***Makes 6.***

BRAIDED RINGS

Your pretzel dough can be fashioned into two large braided rings, perhaps the most impressive pretzels in this book. Follow the instructions for shaping the pretzels, making the following changes: Divide the dough into six equal portions. Shape each into a 30-in/76-cm rope. Apply even pressure as you roll from the center of the dough to the ends to avoid tapering them. Working with three ropes at a time, lay the ropes parallel to each other on your work surface, about 1 in/2.5 cm apart, with the ends pointing toward you. Begin braiding from the center of the ropes to one end, then rotate the dough and finish the other half of the braid. First cross the right rope over the middle rope (note that the right rope then becomes the middle rope), and then the left rope over the middle rope, and then the right rope over the middle, and so on. Repeat this process until you reach the ends of the ropes. Join the ends of the braid to create a flat ring and tuck and pinch the ends together. Braid the other ropes together in the same manner. Proceed as instructed in the recipe. You'll need to prepare the dipping solution in a pot or pan that is at least 12 in/30.5 cm wide. If you have one, use a stainless-steel stove-top wok—the sloped sides make it easy to maneuver the pretzel rings. You'll need two large slotted utensils (preferably two large spatulas) to carefully transfer each ring to and from the dipping solution. Do not attempt to flip the rings over in the solution, just dip the top sides. There is no need to slash the dough before baking. ***Makes 2 large pretzel rings.***

TOPPING OPTIONS

SALT AND SEEDS

Shower pretzels generously with one or more of the following toppings before baking: artisan coarse salt or pretzel salt (see page 15), poppy seeds, caraway seeds, anise seeds, fennel seeds, sesame seeds, sunflower seeds, or pumpkin seeds.

EVERYTHING

Mix together 1 tbsp plus 1 tsp of minced onion, 1 tbsp plus 1 tsp of minced garlic, 1 tbsp plus 1 tsp of sesame seeds, 1 tbsp plus 1 tsp of poppy seeds, and 1 tbsp plus 1 tsp of coarse salt in a small bowl and scatter the mixture over the pretzels. Bake as directed in the recipe.

GARLIC AND PARSLEY

After baking the pretzels for 5 minutes, remove them from the oven and brush them with 1 tbsp of melted butter. Sprinkle the pretzels with 3 tbsp of chopped garlic. Return the pans to the oven, rotating them from front to back and top to bottom, and finish baking as directed in the recipe. After removing the pretzels from the oven, sprinkle them with 3 tbsp of chopped fresh flat-leaf parsley.

PARMIGIANO-REGGIANO CHEESE

Shower the pretzels with ½ cup/60 g of grated fresh Parmigiano-Reggiano cheese and bake them as directed in the recipe.

AGED CHEDDAR CHEESE

Scatter 1½ to 2 cups/120 to 160 g of shredded aged Cheddar cheese over the pretzels and bake them as directed in the recipe.

FETA CHEESE

Scatter 1 cup/150 g of crumbled feta cheese over the pretzels and bake them as directed in the recipe. If the feta is packed in water or whey, be sure to drain it well before topping the pretzels. You may need to press the cheese into the dough to make it stick.

SIGMUND PRETZEL SHOP'S GRUYÈRE AND PAPRIKA

Scatter 1½ to 2 cups/120 to 160 g of shredded Gruyère cheese over the pretzels, and then sprinkle each with a pinch of sweet paprika. Bake the pretzels as directed in the recipe.

PEPPERONI PIZZA

Smear the pretzels with 1 cup/260 g of Tomato-Basil Jam (page 117) or pizza sauce, and then scatter 1½ to 2 cups/120 to 160 g of shredded mozzarella over them. Top the pretzels with a few slices of pepperoni. (The number of slices depends on the pretzel shape and the diameter of the pepperoni. Figure around 2 oz/55 g of pepperoni per batch.) Bake them as directed in the recipe.

CINNAMON-SUGAR

Mix together 1 tsp of ground cinnamon and ¼ cup/50 g of sugar in a small bowl and sprinkle each pretzel generously. Gently press the cinnamon-sugar into the dough to get a good coating. Bake the pretzels as directed in the recipe. Alternatively, you can bake the pretzels plain, and then brush them with 1 tbsp of melted unsalted butter and coat them with cinnamon-sugar after they come out of the oven.

VANILLA ICING

Drizzle this on top of pretzels made with Cinnamon-Raisin Pretzel Dough (page 30) and sprinkled with the Cinnamon-Sugar topping after they've cooled awhile. Or use it as a dip for pretzel bites coated with the sweet sprinkle. Sift 1 cup/100 g of powdered sugar into a medium bowl, whisk in 1 tbsp of water and ¼ tsp of pure vanilla extract, and continue whisking until the sugar has dissolved into a smooth, thick glaze. Add a tiny bit more water if needed, but be sure to keep the icing relatively thick because it will melt on contact with the warm pretzels.

ALMOND STREUSEL

Whisk together ¼ cup/50 g firmly packed light brown sugar, 2 tbsp of all-purpose flour, 1 tsp of ground cinnamon, and ¼ tsp of fine sea salt in a small bowl. Add ¼ cup/30 g of sliced almonds and 2 tbsp of melted unsalted butter, stirring until the mixture is evenly moistened and clumps together. Scatter the streusel topping over the pretzels (on the classic pretzel shape, scatter the streusel on the fattest part of the pretzel only) and press it in, gently flattening the dough, so that it sticks. Reduce the oven temperature to 450°F/230°C/ gas 8 and bake as directed in the master recipe, taking care not to burn the streusel.

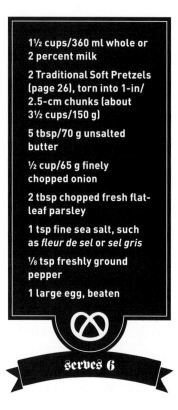

1½ cups/360 ml whole or 2 percent milk

2 Traditional Soft Pretzels (page 26), torn into 1-in/ 2.5-cm chunks (about 3½ cups/150 g)

5 tbsp/70 g unsalted butter

½ cup/65 g finely chopped onion

2 tbsp chopped fresh flat-leaf parsley

1 tsp fine sea salt, such as *fleur de sel* or *sel gris*

⅛ tsp freshly ground pepper

1 large egg, beaten

serves 6

PRETZEL DUMPLINGS

For centuries, German cooks have been creative with their leftover pretzels. Dumplings, a classic pretzel redux, are Bavarian comfort food. The "Franks" (Frank Falcinelli and Frank Castronovo), chef-owners of Prime Meats in Brooklyn, turn their leftover soft pretzels into one large dumpling, which is poached in simmering water. It is then sliced into disks and panfried in butter to accompany beef sauerbraten and braised red cabbage. This is an adaptation of their simple, satisfying recipe. You can also use one of the dough variations for classic soft pretzels, such as Whole-Wheat Pretzel Dough (page 30) or Gluten-Free Pretzel Dough (page 30), or soft pretzels crowned with a savory topping (see page 35), as long as it is not cheese.

Bring the milk to a simmer in a small saucepan over medium-high heat, stirring occasionally. Remove the pan from the heat and add the pretzels. Push the pretzels down to submerge them in the milk, cover the pan, and let stand until most of the milk is absorbed and the pretzels are completely soggy, about 30 minutes.

While the pretzels are soaking, heat a medium sauté pan or skillet over medium heat. Add 1 tbsp of the butter and swirl to coat the pan. Add the onion and cook, stirring occasionally, until softened but not browned, about 7 minutes. Remove from the heat and set aside.

Drain the pretzels in a fine-mesh strainer, pressing on them firmly with a rubber spatula to remove as much milk as possible. Transfer to a large bowl and discard the extracted milk. Scrape the onion into the bowl with the drained pretzels and stir in the parsley, salt, and pepper. Allow the mixture to cool for a few minutes, and then stir in the egg.

Spread out a 14-in/35.5-cm sheet of plastic wrap on your work surface. Spoon half of the dumpling mixture lengthwise down the center of one sheet of plastic and wrap it, shaping the mixture into

a log that is about 2.5 in/6 cm in diameter and about 7 to 9 in/17 to 23 cm long. Twist the ends of the plastic wrap, compressing the dumpling like a sausage. (Don't twist it too tightly, or the dumplings will burst through the plastic wrap while boiling.) Tie the ends with kitchen twine to secure. Wrap the dumpling in another piece of plastic wrap, positioning the seam so it's on the opposite side of the dumpling from the first seam. Wrap the dumpling in a third piece of plastic wrap and twist and tie the ends to secure. Repeat with the remaining dumpling mixture.

Choose a large pot with a diameter that is wider than the length of the dumplings and fill it with at least 4 in/10 cm of water. Bring the water to a simmer over high heat, and then reduce the heat to medium. Add the dumplings to the water and cover the pot. Simmer until the dumplings are slightly firm and cooked through, 25 to 30 minutes, adjusting the heat as needed to maintain a gentle simmer. Turn the dumplings in the water on occasion to cook evenly. Carefully remove them from the water and cool to room temperature. Leave the dumplings in the plastic wrap and refrigerate them until they are cold and firm, at least 2 hours. (The dumplings can be left in the plastic wrap and refrigerated for up to 3 days before frying and serving.)

Preheat the oven to 200°F/95°C and put a rimmed baking sheet inside. Unwrap the dumplings and cut each one into six thick slices. Melt 2 tbsp of the butter in a large skillet over medium-high heat. When it is melted and bubbly, add half of the dumplings and cook, turning once, until browned and crisp, about 5 minutes per side. Transfer the cooked dumplings to the baking sheet in the oven to keep warm. Wipe out the pan, add the remaining 2 tbsp of the butter, and cook the remaining dumplings in the same manner. Serve immediately.

WILD MUSHROOM AND CHESTNUT PRETZEL STUFFING

Got a pretzel surplus? Stuffing is a great way to use up your leftover soft pretzels of any shape, even those with a savory topping (as long as it is not cheesy). This stuffing is rather moist below a crusty top. That's the way I like it, but if you prefer a drier stuffing, you can cut back on the chicken stock by about a quarter. Make this in the fall, when fresh chestnuts and chanterelle mushrooms are in season.

ROASTED CHESTNUTS

1 lb/455 g fresh chestnuts (see Cook's Note)

1 tsp fine sea salt, such as *fleur de sel* or *sel gris*

3 Traditional Soft Pretzels (page 26), cut into ½-in/ 12-mm cubes (about 5½ cups/220 g)

5 tbsp/70 g unsalted butter

1 onion, diced

3 stalks celery, diced

2 large garlic cloves, minced

¼ cup/15 g chopped fresh flat-leaf parsley

1 tbsp minced fresh thyme

1 tbsp minced fresh sage

2 tsp fine sea salt, such as *fleur de sel* or *sel gris*

8 oz/225 g chanterelle mushrooms, cleaned; large ones quartered, medium ones halved, and smaller ones kept whole

2 cups/480 ml homemade chicken or turkey stock or good-quality low-sodium chicken broth

1 cup/240 ml milk

1 large egg, beaten

serves 6 to 8

Position one rack in the upper third and another rack in the lower third of the oven and preheat it to 375°F/190°C/gas 5.

To make the Roasted Chestnuts: Cut a long slit across the rounded side of each chestnut using a serrated knife. Be sure to cut all the way through the shell to reach the nut inside. Put the chestnuts in a medium saucepan and cover with cold water. Add 1 tsp of salt and heat the water over medium-high until it begins to simmer. Immediately drain the chestnuts (do not dry) and transfer them to a small rimmed baking sheet. Roast the chestnuts until most of the shells have burst open and the nut inside is lightly toasted, 25 to 35 minutes. Remove the chestnuts from the oven and cover the pan with a kitchen towel until the chestnuts are cool enough to handle, but still quite warm. Squeeze open the shells and remove the chestnut meat. Some may be more difficult to remove than others, so pop these troublesome chestnuts back into the oven for a few minutes and then try again. Quarter the chestnuts and put them in a large bowl.

While the chestnuts are roasting, spread out the cubed pretzels on a 12-by-17-in/30.5-by-43-cm rimmed baking sheet and put them in the oven to toast until the edges begin to brown, 5 to 10 minutes. Put the pretzel cubes into the bowl with the chestnuts.

Heat a large, heavy, ovenproof skillet, such as a cast-iron one, over medium-high. Melt 3 tbsp of the butter, swirling to coat the pan. Add the onion and celery and cook, stirring occasionally, until the onion begins to brown, 8 to 10 minutes. Stir in the garlic, parsley, thyme, sage, and 2 tsp of salt and cook for 1 minute longer. Dump the onion mixture into the bowl with the pretzels and chestnuts, scraping the skillet clean with a heat-proof silicone spatula.

Return the skillet to medium-high heat and melt 1 tbsp of the remaining butter, swirling to coat the pan. Add the mushrooms and sauté, stirring occasionally, until lightly browned, about 5 minutes. First they will release their liquid, and then, once it evaporates, they will begin to brown. Dump the mushrooms into the bowl with the pretzel mixture. Add the chicken stock, milk, and egg and toss it all together.

Off the heat, grease the skillet thoroughly with the remaining 1 tbsp of butter by swirling it around the bottom and up the sides of the pan. Dump the stuffing mixture back into the skillet and spread it out in an even layer. (The stuffing can be prepared up to 2 days in advance of baking. Store, covered, in the refrigerator. Remove it from the refrigerator about 30 minutes before baking to come to room temperature, and transfer it to the greased cast-iron skillet.) Bake the stuffing until it is brown and crusty on top, about 1 hour. Serve immediately.

....

COOK'S NOTE:
Fresh chestnuts are an autumnal treat. If you're not up to the task of roasting and peeling them yourself, it is just fine to substitute preroasted and peeled chestnuts, which come in a jar or an airtight plastic bag. You'll need about 8½ oz/240 g for this recipe.

Traditional Soft Pretzels dough (page 26)

6 oz/170 g sharp Cheddar cheese, grated (about 2 cups)

2 jalapeño peppers, cut into paper-thin rounds (2/3 cup/80 g)

2 tbsp food-grade lye (see page 20), or 1/4 cup/ 60 g baked baking soda (see page 21)

Coarse salt for topping

makes 6 dozen

JALAPEÑO-CHEDDAR (OR PEANUT BUTTER) PRETZEL BITES

These little jalapeño-and-Cheddar-filled poppers are awesomely spicy. (Kiddos will appreciate the tamer peanut butter variation at the end of the recipe.) Bake a double batch and freeze half so that you'll have them on hand whenever you get the craving, which will be often.

Mix and proof the dough following the instructions on page 26.

Line two 12-by-17-in/30.5-by-43-cm rimmed baking sheets with parchment paper; set aside.

Turn the dough out onto an unfloured work surface and firmly press it down to deflate. Cut it into twelve equal portions. Work with one piece of dough at a time and keep the rest covered with a damp, clean kitchen towel. Pat a piece of dough down with your fingertips to deflate. (If it is sticky, lightly dust the dough and a rolling pin with flour.) Using a rolling pin, roll it into a 4-by-7-in/10-by-17-cm rectangle. Spread a portion of the Cheddar cheese in a narrow line running lengthwise through the center of the rectangle. Scatter five or six jalapeño slices over the cheese. Stretch and fold the long side of the rectangle over the filling to tightly encase it, and then roll up the dough into a cylinder. Pinch the seam and ends to seal. Roll the dough against the work surface, applying light pressure, to smooth out the seam without lengthening the dough. If you need more friction, spray the counter with a little water from a squirt bottle or drizzle a few drops of water and spread it with your hand. Place the stuffed pretzel on one of the prepared baking sheets with the seam-side down and cover it with the damp towel. Repeat this process with the remaining dough and filling, spacing the pretzels out on the baking sheets at least 1 in/2.5 cm apart.

Allow the pretzels to rise at warm room temperature until they have increased in size by about half, 20 to 30 minutes. (The pretzels can be refrigerated at this point, covered tightly with plastic wrap, for up to 8 hours before dipping and baking them.)

At least 20 minutes before baking, position one rack in the upper third and another rack in the lower third of the oven and preheat it to 500°F/260°C/gas 10.

Using the lye or baked baking soda solution, dip the pretzels following the instructions for dipping on page 28. After dipping, cut each stuffed pretzel into six segments using a pizza wheel or sharp knife. Space out the bites on the baking sheets, seam-side down, at least ½ in/12 mm apart, and sprinkle them with coarse salt.

Bake the pretzel bites until they are puffy and brown, 6 to 8 minutes, rotating the pans from front to back and top to bottom halfway through the baking time. Some of the cheese will ooze out of the pretzels, but there will be plenty left inside. (Plus, the crusty cheese on the outside of the pretzels adds to the eating experience.) Transfer the pretzel bites to a rack to cool for 10 minutes before serving. Pretzel bites are best enjoyed the day they are made; ideally warm from the oven or within an hour of being baked. To store them, see page 21.

PEANUT BUTTER PRETZEL BITES
Omit the Cheddar cheese and jalapeños and substitute 1½ cups/ 480 g of creamy peanut butter (get the kind that does not separate or need to be stirred). Spread 2 tbsp of the peanut butter in the center of each rectangle of dough and proceed as directed in the recipe.

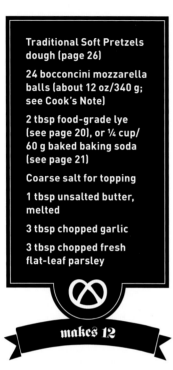

Traditional Soft Pretzels dough (page 26)

24 bocconcini mozzarella balls (about 12 oz/340 g; see Cook's Note)

2 tbsp food-grade lye (see page 20), or ¼ cup/ 60 g baked baking soda (see page 21)

Coarse salt for topping

1 tbsp unsalted butter, melted

3 tbsp chopped garlic

3 tbsp chopped fresh flat-leaf parsley

makes 12

CHEESY PRETZEL PULL-APART ROLLS
WITH GARLIC AND PARSLEY

Garlicky and oozing with mozzarella, these Italian-style pretzel rolls are the perfect companions for a big bowl of spaghetti and a bottle of wine. The rolls are nestled next to each other on the baking sheets and are pulled apart to eat, but you can bake them as individual rolls if you prefer.

Mix and proof the dough following the instructions on page 26.

Line two 12-by-17-in/30.5-by-43-cm rimmed baking sheets with parchment paper; set aside.

Turn the dough out onto an unfloured work surface and press it down firmly to deflate. Divide the dough into twelve equal portions. Work with one piece of dough at a time and keep the rest covered with a damp, clean kitchen towel. Pat a piece of dough down with your fingertips to form a 4-in/10-cm circle. (If it is sticky, lightly dust the work surface and the dough with flour.) Tear two of the mozzarella balls in half and pile them in the center of the dough. Fold over the edges of the circle so that they meet in the middle, encasing the cheese. Pinch the seams together and turn the roll over so that the seam-side is down. Cup your palm over the dough ball and roll it gently yet rapidly against the countertop in a circular motion, without applying much pressure, to smooth out the seams and create a well-shaped sphere. Place the pretzel on one of the prepared baking sheets and cover it with a damp towel. Repeat this process with the remaining dough and mozzarella, spacing out the pretzels on the baking sheets at least 1 in/2.5 cm apart.

Allow the pretzels to rise at warm room temperature until they have increased in size by about half, 20 to 30 minutes. (The pretzels can be refrigerated at this point, covered tightly with plastic wrap, for up to 8 hours before dipping and baking them.)

At least 20 minutes before baking, position one rack in the upper third and another rack in the lower third of the oven and preheat it to 500°F/260°C/gas 10.

Using the lye or baked baking soda solution, dip the pretzels following the instructions for dipping on page 28. Arrange six of the dipped rolls on each baking sheet in a flower pattern, with five rolls forming an outer circle and one roll in the center. Use a sharp paring knife or razor blade to score an X across the top of each roll and sprinkle them with coarse salt.

Bake the pretzels for 5 minutes. Remove the baking sheets from the oven, brush the pretzels with melted butter, and sprinkle them with the garlic. Return the pans to the oven, rotating them from front to back and top to bottom. Bake until the pretzels are brown, about 5 minutes more, watching closely as the garlic can burn easily. Some of the cheese will ooze out of the rolls as they bake, but there will be plenty left in the center. Remove from the oven and sprinkle with parsley. Allow the pretzels to cool for 5 to 10 minutes, and then transfer them to serving platters to pass at the table. The pretzels are best enjoyed warm from the oven on the day they are made. To store the pretzels, see page 21. Reheat cheese-stuffed pretzels in a 350°F/180°C/gas 4 oven for about 8 to 10 minutes, or 10 to 12 minutes if frozen.

COOK'S NOTE
Bocconcini are bite-size fresh mozzarella balls, which are sold by the pound packed in cloudy whey or water at most supermarkets.

12 soft pretzel rolls
(1 batch Traditional
Soft Pretzels, page 26,
made in the shape of
rolls, page 33)

4 tbsp/55 g unsalted
butter, at room
temperature

¼ cup/60 ml Sweet
Bavarian Mustard
(page 108)

1½ lbs/680 g Black Forest
ham, sliced paper-thin

8 oz/225 g Emmentaler
cheese, cut into 12 thin
slices

makes 12

BLACK FOREST HAM AND EMMENTALER PRETZEL ROLLS
WITH SWEET BAVARIAN MUSTARD

I had already concocted this recipe when I visited the Greenbrier resort in West Virginia for a food writers' symposium in the summer of 2011. To my surprise, they too, had thought up the idea, Virginia style. Cute little pretzel rolls piled high with paper-thin slices of Virginia ham and dripping with melted Brie were featured on our lunch buffet one afternoon. So delightful they were, dipped in a cup of tomato soup. This German version makes equally delicious luncheon fare. Top the pretzel rolls with the Everything topping (page 35) for a particularly good variation.

Preheat the oven to 350°F/180°C/gas 4.

Cut the pretzels in half horizontally. Spread the bottom half of each pretzel with butter and the top half with mustard, about 1 tsp of butter and 1 tsp of mustard per pretzel. Pile the ham over the buttered halves of the pretzels, dividing it evenly, and top each with a slice of cheese. Put the tops on the sandwiches and arrange them on a rimmed baking sheet. Bake the minipretzel sandwiches until the cheese is just melted and the ham is warmed through, 6 to 8 minutes. Serve immediately.

PRETZEL CROISSANTS

½ cup/120 ml milk

One ¼-oz/7-g package active dry yeast (2¼ tsp)

3 tbsp firmly packed dark brown sugar

3¼ cups/410 g unbleached all-purpose flour

2 tsp fine sea salt, such as *fleur de sel* or *sel gris*

2 tbsp unsalted butter, cubed, at room temperature, plus more for greasing the bowl

½ cup/120 ml cold pilsner-style beer

BUTTER BLOCK

1½ cups/340 g cold unsalted butter

2 tbsp unbleached all-purpose flour

Unbleached all-purpose flour for dusting

2 tbsp food-grade lye (see page 20), or ¼ cup/60 g baked baking soda (see page 21)

1 egg yolk beaten with 1 tbsp milk

Coarse salt for topping

Sesame seeds or poppy seeds for topping (optional)

makes 12 croissants

Manhattan's City Bakery serves a pretzel croissant that is so famous it has its own website (www.pretzelcroissant.com). Its version of this European delicacy—known as Laugencroissant, or "lye croissant," in German—is topped with sesame seeds, for a nutty savoriness that intrigues and delights in equal measures: Is it a croissant, or is it a pretzel? Whatever it is, it is a marvel of German-French fusion. Many home bakers are hesitant to attempt croissants, which are undoubtedly a time-consuming endeavor. But the procedure is actually easier than you may think and the active time is minimal. The technique of incorporating a chilled block of butter into dough, creating laminated layers, is known as turning. In this recipe, you'll make three turns of the dough by rolling the dough out to a perfect rectangle and then folding it using two letter-style folds and one book-jacket fold. Your efforts will be rewarded with layers and layers of lofty, buttery, flaky pastry enhanced by a crisp, pretzel-flavored crust.

Warm the milk in a small saucepan over low heat until it reaches between 100 and 115°F/38 and 45°C. Immediately remove the pan from the heat and sprinkle in the yeast. Stir in 1 tbsp of the brown sugar until it is dissolved. Allow the yeast to bloom until it is foamy, 5 to 7 minutes. Whisk together the flour, the remaining 2 tbsp of brown sugar, and the fine sea salt in a large bowl. Use your fingertips to rub the 2 tbsp butter into the flour mixture, breaking it up into tiny flour-coated pieces about the size of bread crumbs. Add the foamy yeast mixture and the beer and stir with a rubber spatula to form a shaggy mass. Turn the dough out onto an unfloured work surface and knead it eight to ten times, just until all of the flour is incorporated. (You are trying to prevent the butter from melting from the warmth of your hands, so the dough will not be a smooth,

continued

homogenous mass; rather, flecks of butter should be visible.) The dough will be soft and should be tacky, but not sticky. (If it is sticky, add a little more flour, about 1 tbsp at a time, and knead it in until the dough is smooth. If the dough is not tacky, it is too dry; add water, 1 tsp at a time.)

Choose a bowl that will be large enough to contain the dough after it has doubled in size, and lightly grease it with butter. Transfer the dough to the greased bowl and cover the bowl tightly with plastic wrap. Put the dough in the refrigerator to rise for at least 8 hours, and up to 24 hours, for optimal flavor. For quick croissants, allow the dough to rise in a spot that is at cool room temperature (between 65 and 72°F/18 and 22°C) until it is doubled in size, about 1 hour. It is important that the dough not get warm enough to soften the butter. Note that the flavor of the dough will be much less nuanced if you opt for the quick method.

To make the Butter Block: Beat together the butter and flour in the bowl of a stand mixer fitted with the paddle attachment on medium speed, scraping down the sides of the bowl once or twice, until it forms a smooth mass. This should take less than a minute; you want to make the butter pliable, without beating air into it or melting it. Spread the butter between two large sheets of plastic wrap and use a rolling pin to shape it into an 8-by-9-in/20-by-23-cm rectangle, pushing the butter to the corners and forming straight edges. Use your hands to mold the butter as needed, but work quickly and try not to touch the butter too much so it doesn't melt. The goal is to keep the butter pliable, yet still firm and cool. Wrap the butter block tightly in the plastic wrap and refrigerate it while you roll out the dough.

Lightly dust your work surface and the top of the dough with flour. Roll it out to a 10-by-15-in/25-by-38-cm rectangle that is about ¼ in/ 6 mm thick. Gently pull and stretch the dough, using your hands to form straight edges and sharp corners. Brush any excess flour off the bottom and top of the dough and place the dough so a long edge is facing you, and is parallel to the edge of your work surface. Mentally divide the dough into three 5-in/12-cm sections (you can lightly trace dividing lines in the dough with your finger if you wish).

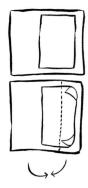

Place the butter block over the two adjacent sections of dough on your right, leaving the left-hand third uncovered and a 1-in/2.5-cm border around the sections that are covered by the butter.

Fold the dough together like a trifold letter: Fold the left section of dough over the center section, covering half of the butter block. Then fold the right section over the center, creating three layers of dough encasing two layers of butter. Pinch together the seams around the edges of the dough. Lightly press the layers together using the rolling pin. This completes what is known as the first turn of the dough. If the butter is still cold and firm, proceed to the next turn. If it seems soft and squishy, wrap the dough in plastic wrap and refrigerate it for 1 hour.

Next, fold the dough together like a book jacket: Working quickly to avoid melting the butter, roll the dough out to form a new 10-by-20-in/25-by-50-cm rectangle, pulling and stretching to form straight edges and sharp corners. Patch any holes where butter may have popped through with a dusting of flour. Brush any excess flour off the bottom and top of the dough and place the dough so a long edge is facing you, and is parallel to the edge of your work surface. Fold the ends of the rectangle into the center, leaving a ¼-in/6-mm gap where they meet. Make sure the edges of the dough stay squared off and perfectly aligned. Fold one side of the dough over the other like a book. Lightly press the layers together using the rolling pin. This completes the second turn. Wrap the dough tightly in plastic wrap and refrigerate it for 1 hour.

For the final turn: Lightly dust your work surface and the top of the dough with flour. Fold the dough together once again like a trifold letter, rolling it out to a 10-by-15-in/25-by-38-cm rectangle and folding it in thirds. Brush off any excess flour. Wrap the dough in plastic wrap and refrigerate it for at least 2 hours and up to 24 hours. Alternatively, you can freeze the dough for 1 hour, but it will be a little more difficult to roll out, cut, and shape. (The dough can be frozen at this point, wrapped tightly in plastic wrap and sealed in a plastic freezer bag, for up to 1 week. Transfer the dough to the refrigerator to defrost overnight before the final shaping.)

continued

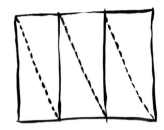

Line two 12-by-17-in/30.5-by-43-cm rimmed baking sheets with parchment paper; set aside.

Lightly dust your work surface and the top of the dough with flour. Roll the dough into a 15-by-18-in/38-by-46-cm rectangle that is about ¼ in/6 mm thick, pulling and stretching to form straight edges and sharp corners. Patch any holes where butter may have popped through with a dusting of flour. Brush any excess flour off the bottom and top of the dough. Cut the rectangle in half lengthwise through the center, creating two sheets of dough that each measure 15 by 9 in/38 by 23 cm. Working with half of the dough at a time, use a pizza cutter or sharp knife to cut each slab of dough into six triangles that are each 5 in/12 mm across at the base and 9 in/23 cm from base to tip. Roll the triangles up, one at a time, beginning at the base and rolling toward the tip. Before completing the roll, gently tug on the tip to elongate it slightly, and then gently press it into the dough. Place the croissants on the prepared baking sheets with the tips tucked under and the ends curved in to form crescent shapes, spacing them at least 2 in/5 cm apart.

Cover the croissants with damp, clean kitchen towels and allow them to rise in a spot that is at cool room temperature (between 65 and 72°F/18 and 22°C) until they have nearly doubled in size and feel spongy, like marshmallows, about 2 hours. Prepare the dipping solution while they rise. Refrigerate the croissants, covered, for at least 20 minutes before dipping.

At least 20 minutes before baking, position one rack in the upper third and another rack in the lower third of the oven and preheat it to 425°F/220°C/gas 7.

Using the lye or baked baking soda solution, dip the pretzels following the instructions for dipping on page 28, but do not heat the solution before dipping the croissants. Just stir it to dissolve the lye or baking soda in cold water. The solution can be prepared several hours in advance. Brush the dipped croissants with the egg wash just to lightly coat the tops. Sprinkle the croissants with coarse salt and sesame seeds or poppy seeds, if using, and bake immediately.

Bake the croissants until they are deeply browned, crispy, and flaky, 14 to 18 minutes, rotating the pans from front to back and top to bottom halfway through the baking time. They should feel light and airy when you pick them up. Transfer the croissants to a rack to cool for 10 minutes before serving. The croissants are best enjoyed the day they are made, ideally within the hour and warm from the oven. To store, see page 21. Reheat pretzel croissants in a 350°F/180°C/gas 4 oven for about 5 minutes, or 8 to 10 minutes if frozen.

Traditional Soft Pretzels
dough (page 26)

8 good-quality hotdogs

2 tbsp food-grade lye
(see page 20), or ¼ cup/
60 g baked baking soda
(see page 21)

Coarse salt for topping

makes 8

PRETZELDOGS

These will rock your pretzel world. Pick up an eight-pack of the best-quality hotdogs you can find and cloak them in a spiral of pretzel dough. Bake them just before heading out for a summer picnic, or take them to your next dodgeball tournament. Swoonworthy, hot or at room temperature, pretzeldogs should be dunked in Spiced Aquavit Mustard (page 112) or Nacho Cheese (page 116).

Mix and proof the dough following the instructions on page 26.

Line two 12-by-17-in/30.5-by-43-cm rimmed baking sheets with parchment paper; set aside.

Turn the dough out onto an unfloured work surface and firmly press it down to deflate. Cut it into eight equal portions. Work with one piece of dough at a time and keep the rest covered with a damp, clean kitchen towel. Gently pat the dough down with your fingertips to form a rough rectangle. Roll it up tightly lengthwise, forming it into a little loaf. Pinch the seam together. Shape the dough into a rope 20 in/50 cm long by rolling it underneath your palms while applying gentle, even pressure, working from the center of the dough out to the ends. Place a hotdog at one end of the rope, perpendicular to the dough, about ¼ in/6 mm from the tip of the hotdog. Roll the hotdog up tightly, cloaking it in a spiral of pretzel dough. Be sure to overlap the long edges of dough as you roll, and tuck in the ends. Place the pretzeldog on one of the prepared baking sheets with the tucked-in ends down and cover it with a damp towel. Repeat this process with the remaining dough and hotdogs, arranging the pretzeldogs at least 2 in/5 cm apart.

Allow the pretzels to rise at warm room temperature until they have increased in size by about half, 20 to 30 minutes. (The pretzels can be refrigerated at this point, covered tightly with plastic wrap, for up to 8 hours before dipping and baking them.)

At least 20 minutes before baking, position one rack in the upper third and another rack in the lower third of the oven and preheat it to 500°F/260°C/gas 10.

Using the lye or baked baking soda solution, dip the pretzels following the instructions for dipping on page 28. Sprinkle the pretzeldogs with coarse salt and bake immediately.

Bake the pretzeldogs until they are deep mahogany in color, 8 to 12 minutes, rotating the pans from front to back and top to bottom after 5 minutes of baking. Transfer them to a rack to cool for 5 minutes before serving. The pretzeldogs are best enjoyed the day they are made; ideally warm from the oven or within an hour of being baked. To store the pretzels, see page 21. Reheat the pretzeldogs in a 350°F/180°C/gas 4 oven for about 10 minutes, or 15 to 20 minutes if frozen.

Traditional Soft Pretzels dough (page 26)

Unbleached all-purpose flour for dusting

3 tbsp Sweet Bavarian Mustard (page 108) or the mustard of your choice

48 cocktail franks

2 tbsp food-grade lye (see page 20), or ¼ cup/ 60 g baked baking soda (see page 21)

Coarse salt for topping (optional)

Poppy seeds for topping (optional)

makes 4 dozen

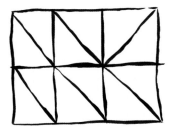

PIGS IN PRETZEL BLANKETS

When I brought these adorable little two-bite snacks to a barbecue one summer, my girlfriends and I had a laugh brainstorming about what to call them. Piggies Wrapped in Pretzel Blankies, Swine in Duvets, and Pretzel-Swaddled Piglets were all eliminated. We had a heck of a time conveying that these are not merely pigs in a blanket—that moniker just doesn't express the lovely enhancement that pretzel dough gives to this old-school hors d'oeuvre.

Mix and proof the dough following the instructions on page 26.

Line two 12-by-17-in/30.5-by-43-cm rimmed baking sheets with parchment paper; set aside.

Turn the dough out onto a lightly floured work surface and firmly press it down to deflate. Cut it into four equal portions. Work with one piece of dough at a time and keep the rest covered with a damp, clean kitchen towel. Gently pat the dough down with your fingertips and then use a rolling pin to flatten it out to an 8-in/20-cm square. Lightly dust the rolling pin and the dough with flour if the dough is sticky. Gently pull and stretch the dough, using your hands to form straight edges and sharp corners. Brush any excess flour off the bottom and top of the dough. Use a pizza wheel or knife to cut the dough in half through the center, and then cut each half into six triangles for a total of twelve triangular strips of dough. Spread a thin smear of mustard at the base (the widest part) of each triangle. Place a cocktail frank over the mustard and roll it up in the dough, gently pushing in the tip to seal. Place the pretzels on one of the prepared baking sheets with the points tucked under, and cover them with damp towels. Repeat this process with the remaining dough and franks, arranging the pretzels at least 2 in/5 cm apart.

continued

Allow the pretzels to rise at warm room temperature until they have increased in size by about half, 20 to 30 minutes. (The pretzels can be refrigerated at this point, covered tightly with plastic wrap, for up to 8 hours before dipping and baking them.)

At least 20 minutes before baking, position one rack in the upper third and another rack in the lower third of the oven and preheat it to 500°F/260°C/gas 10.

Using the lye or baked baking soda solution, dip the pretzels following the instructions for dipping on page 28. Sprinkle the dipped pigs in a blanket with coarse salt or poppy seeds or both, as you desire. Bake them immediately.

Bake the pigs in a blanket until they are deep mahogany in color, 8 to 12 minutes, rotating the pans from front to back and top to bottom after 5 minutes of baking. Transfer them to a rack to cool for 5 minutes before serving. The pretzels are best enjoyed the day they are made; ideally warm from the oven or within an hour of being baked. To store the pretzels, see page 21. Reheat them in a 350°F/180°C/gas 4 oven for about 8 minutes, or 12 to 15 minutes if frozen.

PHILLY CHEESESTEAK PRETZEL POCKETS

Traditional Soft Pretzels dough (page 26)

PEPPER AND ONION FILLING

2 tbsp extra-virgin olive oil

1 green bell pepper, seeded, deribbed, and thinly sliced

1 onion, thinly sliced

½ tsp fine sea salt, such as *fleur de sel* or *sel gris*

Unbleached all-purpose flour for dusting

8 oz/225 g thinly sliced roast beef (from a leftover roast or purchased at a deli counter)

8 slices provolone cheese (about 8 oz/225 g)

2 tbsp food-grade lye (see page 20) or ¼ cup/ 60 g baked baking soda (see page 21)

Coarse salt for topping

makes 8

When I was researching this book, I learned of an extraordinary pretzel stand called Miller's Twist, located in the Reading Terminal Market in Philadelphia. My local tour guides—my aunt and uncle Jane and Phil Rapone and my cousin Lauren Clapper—took me there. It was breakfast and ahead was a long day of touring Pennsylvania Dutch Country in search of America's first pretzel bakery (that's another story). But Miller's case was already lined with buttery, glistening pretzeldogs and an array of cheese-and-meat-filled pretzel pockets. Since I firmly believe in the sentiment "when in Rome," I selected a Philly cheesesteak–stuffed pretzel. Upon tasting it, I simply had to add it to my list of recipes to develop for this book. Like those other pockets you see in the grocer's freezer case, you can freeze these and pop them in the oven for a quick snack or dinner.

Mix and proof the dough following the instructions on page 26.

To make the Pepper and Onion Filling: Heat a large cast-iron skillet or a heavy sauté pan over medium-high heat. Add the olive oil and swirl to coat the pan. When the oil is shimmering-hot, add the bell pepper, onion, and salt and sauté, stirring occasionally, until the vegetables are tender and evenly browned, about 15 minutes. Remove the pan from the heat and transfer the vegetable mixture to a plate to cool to room temperature. The pepper and onion can be cooked up to 1 day in advance and stored, covered, in the refrigerator until needed.

Line two 12-by-17-in/30.5-by-43-cm rimmed baking sheets with parchment paper; set aside.

Turn the dough out onto a lightly floured work surface and firmly press it down to deflate. Cut it into eight equal portions. Work

continued

with one piece of dough at a time and keep the rest covered with a damp, clean kitchen towel. Pat the dough down with your fingertips to form a rough rectangle. Using a lightly floured rolling pin, form the dough into a large rectangle, about 6½ in/16.5 cm wide and 7½ in/19 cm long. With one of the shorter sides facing you, layer a portion of the filling ingredients over the bottom half of the dough (the half that is closest to you) in the following order, keeping a 1-in/2.5-cm border around the edge: roast beef down first, then the pepper and onion filling, and then 1 slice of provolone on top. Brush the edges of the dough with water and fold the empty half of the rectangle over the filling, gently stretching it to align the edges of dough. Pinch the seams together to seal tightly. Press the tines of a fork into the dough along the seam to seal and score the edge. Place the pretzel pocket on one of the prepared baking sheets and cover it with a damp towel. Repeat this process with the remaining dough and filling, arranging the pretzels at least 1 in/2.5 cm apart.

Allow the pretzels to rise at warm room temperature, about 20 minutes. (The pretzels can be refrigerated at this point, covered tightly with plastic wrap, for up to 8 hours before dipping and baking them.)

At least 20 minutes before baking, position one rack in the upper third and another rack in the lower third of the oven and preheat it to 500°F/260°C/gas 10.

Using the lye or baked baking soda solution, dip the pretzels following the instructions for dipping on page 28. Sprinkle the dipped pockets with coarse salt. It may be necessary to press the edges with the tines of a fork to seal them before baking.

Bake the pretzel pockets until they are deep mahogany in color, 8 to 12 minutes, rotating the pans from front to back and top to bottom after 5 minutes of baking. Some of the cheese may ooze out, but there will be plenty left inside the pockets and the crispy cheese just adds to their enjoyment. Transfer them to a rack to cool for 5 minutes before serving. Pretzel pockets are best enjoyed hot from the oven on the day they are made. To store the pockets, see page 21. Reheat in a 350°F/180°C/gas 4 oven for 10 to 12 minutes, or 15 to 20 minutes if frozen.

4 Philadelphia-style soft pretzels (½ batch Traditional Soft Pretzels, page 26, made in the Philadelphia-style shape, page 31)

4 tbsp/55 g unsalted butter, at room temperature

4 oz/115 g chèvre (soft, fresh goat cheese)

½ cup/130 g Tomato-Basil Jam (page 117)

3½ oz/100 g cold Taleggio cheese, rind removed and thinly sliced

3½ oz/100 g Fontina Val d'Aosta cheese or another good Italian Fontina, shredded

makes 4

PRETZEL GRILLED CHEESE
WITH TOMATO-BASIL JAM

Two velvety Italian melting cheeses, Fontina and Taleggio, and creamy-soft goat cheese make an ideal combination for the quint-essential grilled cheese sandwich, cooked panini-style between pretzel halves.

Preheat the oven to 200ºF/95ºC and put a rimmed baking sheet inside.

Cut the pretzels in half horizontally and spread the cut sides with butter. Heat a large cast-iron skillet or a heavy sauté pan over medium heat. Working in two batches, toast the pretzels in the hot skillet, buttered-side down, until golden and crusty, about 5 minutes.

Spread the toasted side of the bottom half of each pretzel with a portion of the goat cheese, and spread the toasted side of the top half with the Tomato-Basil Jam. Layer the Taleggio on top of the goat cheese, and pile on the shredded Fontina. Sandwich the pretzel halves together.

Put the skillet over medium-low heat. When it's hot, put two of the sandwiches in the skillet and place another heavy skillet on top of them to smash them down, griddling the crust and melting the cheese, 2 to 3 minutes. When the bottom crust is crispy, flip the sandwiches to cook on the other side until the cheese is completely melted, 2 to 3 minutes more. Transfer the grilled cheese to the baking sheet in the oven while you cook the other two sandwiches. When they are all griddled, serve immediately.

RUSSIAN DRESSING

¼ cup/60 ml mayonnaise

1 tbsp ketchup

2 tsp minced fresh flat-leaf parsley

1 tsp prepared horseradish

1 tsp grated onion

1 tsp minced dill pickles

Dash of Worcestershire sauce

4 caraway-rye Philadelphia-style soft pretzels (½ batch Traditional Soft Pretzels, page 26, made with the Caraway-Rye Pretzel Dough variation, page 30, in the Philadelphia-style shape, page 31)

4 tbsp/55 g unsalted butter, at room temperature

2 cups/320 g Quick Sauerkraut (see page 66) or store-bought sauerkraut

1½ lbs/680 g thinly sliced corned beef brisket

6 oz/170 g Gruyère cheese, cut into 12 thin slices

makes 4

PRETZEL REUBENS ON CARAWAY-RYE

A good Reuben is my favorite sandwich. Reubens on pretzel bread? Yes, I've found heaven. There's an art to constructing the perfect Reuben, and the first step is to bake the Caraway-Rye Pretzel Dough variation of Traditional Soft Pretzels in the Philadelphia-style shape. As always, buy the best-quality ingredients to make these sandwiches. If you are into fermenting your own cabbage to make homemade sauerkraut, this recipe is for you. For the rest of us, Quick Sauerkraut is the answer, and store-bought is fine, too, but preferably from a deli case rather than a jar. Good corned beef is also crucial. My local delicatessen makes excellent corned beef brisket in-house. Use the best you can find—the fattier, the better.

To make the Russian Dressing: Whisk together the mayonnaise, ketchup, parsley, horseradish, onion, pickles, and Worcestershire sauce in a small bowl. The dressing can be made up to 5 days in advance and refrigerated, covered, until needed.

Preheat the oven to 200°F/95°C and put a rimmed baking sheet inside.

Slice the pretzels in half horizontally and spread the cut sides with butter. Heat a large cast-iron skillet or a heavy sauté pan over medium heat. Working in two batches, toast the pretzels in the hot skillet, buttered-side down, until golden and crusty, about 5 minutes. Meanwhile, warm the sauerkraut in a small saucepan over medium-low heat or in the microwave. Drain the sauerkraut well before topping the sandwiches.

continued

Spread both of the toasted sides of each pretzel with a generous smear of the Russian Dressing. Layer a portion of the filling ingredients on the bottom half of each pretzel in the following order: Spread the sauerkraut out first, then pile on the corned beef, and then fan out three slices of Gruyère cheese on top. Sandwich the pretzel halves together.

Put the skillet back on medium-low heat. When it's hot, put two of the sandwiches in the skillet and place another heavy skillet on top of them to smash them down, griddling the crust, 2 to 3 minutes. When the bottom crust is crispy, flip the sandwiches and cook on the other side until the cheese is completely melted, 2 to 3 minutes more. Transfer the grilled Reubens to the baking sheet in the oven while you cook the other two sandwiches. When they are all griddled, cut the Reubens in half on a diagonal and serve immediately.

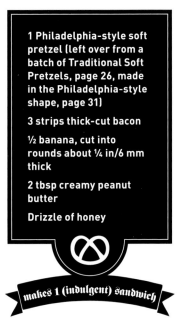

1 Philadelphia-style soft pretzel (left over from a batch of Traditional Soft Pretzels, page 26, made in the Philadelphia-style shape, page 31)

3 strips thick-cut bacon

½ banana, cut into rounds about ¼ in/6 mm thick

2 tbsp creamy peanut butter

Drizzle of honey

makes 1 (indulgent) sandwich

THE ELVIS—
PEANUT BUTTER,
BANANA, AND BACON
PRETZELWICH

After your long Saturday night of partying, Elvis has your Sunday-morning cure. The King was known to have an affinity for this gut-bomb-of-a-sandwich, but my, how the decadence is amped up when it's presented between two slices of sexy pretzel bread.

Preheat the oven to 350°F/180°C/gas 4. Slice the pretzel in half horizontally. Have ready two paper towel–lined plates.

Heat a medium to large skillet over medium-high heat. When the pan is hot, add the bacon and cook until crisp on the edges but still a little fatty and supple in the center, turning once, 5 to 8 minutes. Transfer the bacon to one of the paper towel–lined plates; set aside.

Add the sliced banana to the pan and fry it in the rendered bacon fat, turning once, until lightly browned, 1 to 2 minutes per side. Transfer the fried banana to the other paper towel–lined plate, dab off the excess grease, and then discard the paper towel. (The bananas will stick to the paper towel if they're left on it too long.)

Pour off all but about 1 tbsp of the fat from the pan and return it to medium-high heat. Toast the cut sides of the pretzel in the bacon drippings until crisp and golden brown, about 5 minutes.

Spread the bottom half of the griddled pretzel with the peanut butter. Layer the bananas over the peanut butter and drizzle them with honey. Arrange the bacon over the bananas and top with the other half of the pretzel. Put the sandwich on a baking sheet and heat it in the oven to refresh the crust and warm through, about 5 minutes. Eat immediately with a tall glass of cold milk.

BAVARIAN "BREAKFAST" SANDWICHES

makes 6

Though a pretzel filled with sausage, mustard, and sauerkraut may sound like lunch, in Bavaria this is indeed breakfast. Okay, maybe this is a slightly Americanized sandwich-y version. Nevertheless, it is true that in southern Germany, Weisswurst— white sausages made of veal, pork, parsley, and spices—are akin to breakfast links, served with sweet mustard and a warm, soft pretzel before the noon bells ring. And, of course, a beer. If you turned to this page expecting to find a pretzel McMuffin, here's what you do: Fry up some bacon, crack an egg in the pan drippings, and load it into a pretzel roll. There, you have two recipes in one.

To make the Quick Sauerkraut: Heat a large Dutch oven or another large, heavy pot over medium heat. Add the oil and swirl to coat the bottom of the pot. Add the cabbage and stir in the salt. Cover and cook, stirring occasionally, until the cabbage is wilted and tender, about 12 minutes. Uncover and cook until most of the liquid has evaporated from the bottom of the pot, about 5 minutes more. Add the beer, vinegar, brown sugar, and caraway seeds and bring the mixture to a boil over medium-high heat. Reduce the heat to low, cover, and simmer until the cabbage is extremely tender, 25 to 30 minutes. Taste and adjust the seasoning, adding more salt, vinegar, or brown sugar, as you like.

Nestle the sausages in the pot with the sauerkraut so that they are mostly covered by the cabbage and liquid. Cover and simmer until the sausages are warmed through, 8 to 10 minutes.

Cut each pretzel roll in half horizontally, so that it's cut almost all the way through but the two halves are still connected (like a hot-dog bun). Spread both halves of each pretzel with mustard. Pull the sausages from the sauerkraut and stuff them in the rolls. Top each roll with a heap of sauerkraut, draining off the excess liquid. Serve immediately with cold *Weissbier* for drinking.

The leftover Quick Sauerkraut will keep for a week or more, covered, in the refrigerator. Rewarm it in a saucepan over medium-low heat.

COOK'S NOTE:

Weisswurst sausages have a fine texture and somewhat gamy flavor, which is splendidly balanced by the acidic sauerkraut. Look for them at a German delicatessen, or substitute bratwurst instead. If you purchase uncooked sausages, be sure to cook them through completely in the sauerkraut, about 15 minutes, before serving.

½ batch Traditional Soft Pretzels dough (see Cook's Note, page 29)

Peanut or canola oil for deep-frying

Cinnamon-Sugar topping (page 35)

makes 12 minipretzels

FRIED PRETZELS
WITH CINNAMON-SUGAR

Denser than beignets and doughnuts, though equally delicious, deep-fried pretzel dough tossed in cinnamon and sugar makes a whimsical breakfast treat. The pretzels also make for a fun ending to an informal dinner party. Served with Dark Chocolate–Peanut Butter Dunk (page 123), they are reminiscent of Spanish churros y chocolate, *with a twist . . . literally.*

Mix and proof the dough following the instructions on page 26.

Line a 12-by-17-in/30.5-by-43-cm baking sheet with parchment paper; set aside.

Turn the dough out onto an unfloured work surface and firmly press it down to deflate. Cut it into twelve equal portions. Work with one piece of dough at a time and keep the rest covered with a damp, clean kitchen towel. Pat the dough down with your fingertips to form a rough rectangle. Tightly roll it up lengthwise into a cylinder. Shape the dough into a rope 16 in/40.5 cm long by rolling it against the work surface, working from the center of the rope out to the ends. Apply a little more pressure as you near the ends to taper them slightly. If you need more friction, spray the counter with a little water from a squirt bottle or drizzle a few drops of water and spread it with your hand.

Position the dough rope into a U shape with the ends pointing away from you. Holding one of the ends in each hand, cross the ends. Form the classic pretzel shape by folding the ends down and pressing them into the bottom of the U at about 4 and 8 o'clock, allowing about ⅛ in/3 mm of the ends to overhang. Place the pretzel on the prepared baking sheet and cover it with a damp towel. Repeat this process with the remaining dough, spacing the pretzels out on the baking sheet at least 1 in/2.5 cm apart.

continued

Allow the pretzels to rise at warm room temperature until they have increased in size by about half, 20 to 30 minutes. (The pretzels can be refrigerated at this point, covered tightly with plastic wrap, for up to 8 hours before dipping and frying them.)

Prepare the frying oil while they rise, or at least 20 minutes before baking.

Pour 2 in/5 cm of oil into a deep, heavy pot. (Or use an electric deep-fryer, following the manufacturer's instructions for heating the oil.) Heat the oil until the temperature registers 350°F/180°C on a deep-fat thermometer. Have ready a large skimmer or slotted spoon. Set a wire cooling rack over a sheet of aluminum foil near the stove top to collect the pretzels as they are fried.

Carefully slide three or four of the pretzels into the hot oil at a time. Keep in mind that the pretzels will puff as they fry, so be sure not to crowd the pot. Fry until the pretzels are puffy, crisp, and golden, flipping them in the oil to brown evenly, about 2 minutes total. (Adjust your heat to maintain the oil at 350°F/180°C while frying.) With the skimmer, remove the pretzels from the fat, allow the excess fat to drain, and transfer them to the cooling rack. If the oil drops below 350°F/180°C, allow it to return to the proper temperature before frying the next batch; otherwise the pretzels will absorb too much oil and be greasy. Continue until all of the pretzels are fried.

Put a few of the fried pretzels at a time into a large bowl and sprinkle them with a generous amount of the Cinnamon-Sugar, tossing to coat evenly. Serve immediately.

PRETZEL BREAD PUDDING
WITH SALTED CARAMEL SAUCE

3 Traditional Soft Pretzels (page 26), torn into 1-in/2.5-cm chunks (about 5½ cups/220 g)

4 large eggs plus 2 egg yolks

1 vanilla bean

3 cups/720 ml milk

⅔ cup/130 g sugar

2 tbsp bourbon

¼ tsp fine sea salt (optional; include only if the pretzels are not already topped with salt)

Nonstick cooking spray for the ramekins

1 cup Salted Caramel Sauce (page 121)

Powdered sugar for dusting the puddings

serves 6

Bread pudding is a classic rescue for stale loaves headed for the compost heap. Your homemade soft pretzels deserve this sweet final hurrah, too. Use leftover soft pretzels of any shape for this recipe. Cinnamon-raisin pretzels (see page 30) are especially delicious here. If you don't have six ramekins, bake one large pudding in a 2-qt/2-L baking dish (see photo on page 72) and increase the baking time to 40 to 50 minutes. Serve the pudding warm from the oven at breakfast or for dessert.

Position a rack in the center of the oven and preheat it to 325°F/165°C/gas 3.

Spread out the cubed pretzels on a 12-by-17-in/30.5-by-43-cm rimmed baking sheet and put them in the oven until they are completely dried out, without browning, 7 to 12 minutes. Set aside to cool.

Beat the eggs and yolks in a large bowl. Slit the vanilla bean down the center lengthwise and use the back of the knife to scrape out the seeds into the bowl with the eggs. (Reserve the pod for another use.) Whisk in the milk, sugar, bourbon, and salt, if using. Stir the pretzels into the custard mixture. Press a sheet of plastic wrap against the surface of the custard and place a heavy plate on top to weigh it down so that the pretzel cubes are completely submerged. Refrigerate the weighted pudding overnight, or until the pretzels are completely soggy with custard, at least 6 hours.

Position a rack in the center of the oven and preheat it to 325°F/165°C/gas 3 at least 20 minutes before you plan to bake the puddings. Coat six 6-oz/180-ml ceramic ramekins or ovenproof custard cups with nonstick cooking spray. Loosely pack the bread pudding

continued

into the ramekins and pour in any remaining custard, dividing it evenly. Arrange the puddings in a roasting pan that is large enough so that the ramekins are not touching. Fill the roasting pan with enough hot water so that it comes halfway up the sides of the ramekins. (I heat a teapot full of water, which will pour into the roasting pan with ease.)

Transfer the roasting pan to the oven, taking care not to splash the water into the puddings. Bake the puddings until the tops are lightly browned and the custard is set, 22 to 28 minutes. To test for doneness, tap the sides of the ramekins and see if the custard jiggles loosely like gelatin. If it does, then it is set and the custard will be creamy and soft. (If you wait too long, the puddings will puff up dramatically, like soufflés, and the custard will be firm.) Remove the pan from the oven at once.

Carefully remove the puddings from the water bath and allow them to cool for 5 minutes before serving. Heat the caramel sauce on the stove top, or microwave it in 20-second increments until hot. Put the bread puddings on individual plates and drizzle them with the sauce, allowing it to drip down the sides of the ramekins. Dust with powdered sugar and serve immediately. Pass the remaining caramel sauce at the table.

Leftover bread pudding can be refrigerated for up to 4 days and reheated, covered with aluminum foil, in a 325°F/165°C/gas 3 oven until warmed through, 15 to 20 minutes.

HARD PRETZELS

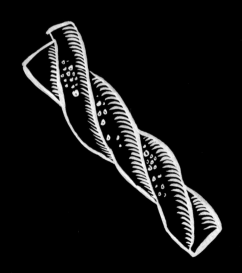

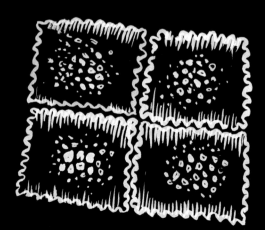

Hard pretzels are a craveable American creation. They hail from the Pennsylvania Dutch Country, where long ago German immigrants reimagined the soft pretzels from their homeland, turning them into fat, crunchy little cracker breads. Traditionally they were kneaded and shaped by hand, of course, and baked to a deep, dark brown in wood-burning ovens. Today there are very few bakeries that still make them by hand, though the results are significantly more delicious. Make the first recipe in this chapter to see what a hard pretzel is supposed to taste like. Throughout the following pages, you'll find crunchy pretzel-inspired recipes, as well as classic and new ideas for turning your homemade hard pretzels (or store-bought versions) into novel creations.

PENNSYLVANIA DUTCH HARD PRETZELS

One ¼-oz/7-g package active dry yeast (2¼ tsp)

1 cup/240 ml warm water (between 100 and 115°F/ 38 and 45°C)

1 tbsp barley malt syrup (see page 15) or 1 tbsp firmly packed dark brown sugar

3½ cups/440 g unbleached all-purpose flour

2 tbsp unsalted butter, cubed, at room temperature, plus more for greasing the bowl

2 tsp fine sea salt, such as *fleur de sel* or *sel gris*

2 tbsp food-grade lye (see page 20), or ¼ cup/ 60 g baked baking soda (see page 21)

Coarse salt for topping

makes 24 classic pretzels

A happy culinary accident (see page 10), hard pretzels are one of America's first salty, crunchy snack foods. Traditional recipes for hard pretzels are fat-free, but I find that a few pats of butter added to the dough lend the pretzels an extra-special crispiness and a savory flavor. If you prefer the drier crunch of the traditional style, omit the butter. For pretzel rods, see the variation at the end of the recipe.

Sprinkle the yeast over the warm water in the bowl of a stand mixer or in a large bowl. Add the barley malt syrup, stirring until it is dissolved. Allow the yeast to bloom until it is foamy, 5 to 7 minutes. Add the flour, butter, and fine sea salt and stir to form a shaggy mass. Attach the bowl and the dough hook to the stand mixer and begin kneading on medium-low speed. After about 1 minute the dough will form a smooth ball. The dough should be quite firm and may be slightly tacky, but not sticky. (If it is sticky, add a little more flour, about 1 tbsp at a time, and knead it in until the dough is smooth. If the dough is too dry to come together, add more water, 1 tsp at a time.) Continue kneading the dough on medium-low speed until it is elastic, 5 to 7 minutes. Alternatively, turn the shaggy dough out onto an unfloured work surface and knead it by hand.

Choose a bowl that will be large enough to contain the dough after it has doubled in size, and lightly grease it with butter. Transfer the dough to the greased bowl and cover the bowl tightly with plastic wrap. Put the dough in the refrigerator to rise for at least 8 hours, and up to 24 hours, for optimal flavor.

Line two 12-by-17-in/30.5-by-43-cm rimmed baking sheets with parchment paper; set aside.

continued

Turn the dough out onto an unfloured work surface and press it down to deflate. Cut it into four equal portions, and divide each portion into six small chunks of dough. Work with one piece of dough at a time and keep the rest covered with a damp, clean kitchen towel. Pat a piece of dough down with your fingertips to form a rough rectangle. Roll it up tightly, beginning with a long side, into a cylinder. Shape the dough into a rope 18 in/46 cm long by rolling it against the work surface, using your palms and working from the center of the rope out to the ends. Apply a little more pressure as you get closer to the ends to taper them slightly. If you need more friction, spray the counter with a little water from a squirt bottle or drizzle a few drops of water and spread it with your hand. It is important that the dough be rolled out to the correct length, or it will be too thick to harden during baking.

Position the dough rope into a U shape, with the ends pointing away from you. Holding an end in each hand, cross the ends and then cross them again. Fold the ends down and press them into the U at about 4 and 8 o'clock, allowing about $1/8$ in/3 mm of the ends to overhang. Place the pretzel on one of the prepared baking sheets and cover it with a damp towel. Repeat this process with the remaining dough, arranging the pretzels at least 1 in/2.5 cm apart and covering them with a damp towel.

When the first baking sheet is filled with twelve pretzels, transfer it to the refrigerator while you shape the rest of the pretzels to prevent the first batch from overproofing. When all the pretzels are shaped, leave both trays, covered, at warm room temperature to rise until the pretzels have doubled in size, 30 to 40 minutes. (The pretzels can be refrigerated at this point, covered tightly with plastic wrap, for up to 8 hours before dipping and baking them.)

At least 20 minutes before baking, position one rack in the upper third and another rack in the lower third of the oven and preheat it to 325°F/165°C/gas 3.

Using the lye or baked baking soda solution, dip the pretzels following the instructions for dipping on page 28, working in batches of four to six pretzels at a time, depending on the size of your pot. After dipping, sprinkle the pretzels with coarse salt. Bake them immediately.

Bake the pretzels for 25 minutes, and then rotate the pans from front to back and top to bottom. Continue baking until the pretzels are mahogany in color and completely hard throughout. This could take anywhere from 25 to 40 minutes more, but rely on the visual and textural cues rather than the time. To test a pretzel for doneness, remove one from the oven and break it in half. If the center is still a little chewy, continue baking. If the color is deep brown but the pretzels are not done inside, remove the trays from the oven and allow them to cool to room temperature while you reduce the oven temperature to 300°F/150°C/gas 2. Return the pretzels to the oven to finish hardening to a crisp. Test a pretzel after about 10 minutes, and in 5-minute increments after that. When they are hard, transfer the pretzels to a cooling rack. Once they are completely cooled, store them in an airtight container for up to 2 weeks.

HARD PRETZEL RODS

Divide the dough into forty-eight pieces. Roll the dough ropes out to 8-in/20-cm sticks without tapering the ends, and proceed as directed in the recipe. The total baking time will be reduced to 45 to 55 minutes, or until they are deep brown and hard throughout.

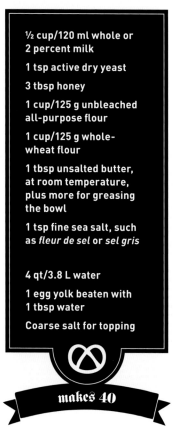

½ cup/120 ml whole or 2 percent milk

1 tsp active dry yeast

3 tbsp honey

1 cup/125 g unbleached all-purpose flour

1 cup/125 g whole-wheat flour

1 tbsp unsalted butter, at room temperature, plus more for greasing the bowl

1 tsp fine sea salt, such as *fleur de sel* or *sel gris*

4 qt/3.8 L water

1 egg yolk beaten with 1 tbsp water

Coarse salt for topping

makes 40

HONEY-WHEAT PRETZEL TWISTS

Snack on these to satisfy your craving for sweet, salty, and crunchy. Unlike the pale, sugar-laden honey-wheat pretzel twists sold in bags at the grocery store, these are subtly sweetened with fragrant honey, deeply browned, and snappy. They are dipped in a plain water bath, rather than lye, because the honey provides sufficient flavor and helps with the browning.

Warm the milk in a small saucepan over low heat until it reaches between 100 and 115°F/38 and 45°C. Immediately pour the warm milk into the bowl of a stand mixer or a large bowl and sprinkle in the yeast. Add 1 tbsp of the honey, stirring until it is dissolved. Allow the yeast to bloom until it is foamy, 5 to 7 minutes. Add the remaining 2 tbsp of honey, the all-purpose flour, whole-wheat flour, butter, and fine sea salt to the yeast mixture and stir to form a shaggy mass. Attach the bowl and the dough hook to the stand mixer and begin kneading on medium-low speed. After about 1 minute the dough will form a smooth ball. The dough should be quite firm and may be slightly tacky, but not sticky. (If it is sticky, add a little more flour, about 1 tbsp at a time, and knead it in until the dough is smooth. If the dough is too dry to come together, add more water, 1 tsp at a time.) Continue kneading the dough on medium speed until it is elastic, 5 to 7 minutes. Alternatively, turn the shaggy dough out onto an unfloured work surface and knead it by hand.

Choose a bowl that will be large enough to contain the dough after it has doubled in size, and lightly grease it with butter. Transfer the dough to the greased bowl and cover the bowl tightly with plastic wrap. Set the dough aside at room temperature (in a warm spot) to rise until it has doubled in size, 1½ to 2 hours.

Line two 12-by-17-in/30.5-by-43-cm rimmed baking sheets with parchment paper; set aside.

Turn the dough out onto an unfloured work surface and press it down to deflate. Cut it into four equal portions, and divide each portion into five small chunks of dough. Work with one piece of dough at a time and keep the rest covered with a damp, clean kitchen towel. Pat a piece of dough down with your fingertips and then roll it up tightly, beginning with a long side, into a cylinder. Shape the dough into a rope 20 in/50 cm long by rolling it against the work surface with your palms, working from the center of the dough to the ends and applying light, even pressure to avoid tapering them. If you need more friction, spray the counter with a little water from a squirt bottle or drizzle a few drops of water and spread it with your hand. It is important that the dough be rolled out to the correct length or it will be too thick to harden while baking. Roll another piece of dough into a rope in this same manner. Twist the two dough ropes together sixteen times, spacing the twists out evenly. Place the twisted dough rope on one of the prepared baking sheets and cover it with a damp towel. Repeat this process with the remaining dough, spacing out the ropes on the baking sheets at least 1 in/2.5 cm apart and covering them with a damp towel.

When the first baking sheet is filled with five twisted ropes, transfer the tray to the refrigerator while you shape the rest of the pretzels to prevent the first batch from overproofing. When all the pretzels are shaped, you will have ten twisted ropes. Place both trays out, covered, at warm room temperature to rise until they have doubled in size, 30 to 40 minutes. (The pretzels can be refrigerated at this point, covered tightly with plastic wrap, for up to 8 hours before dipping and baking them.)

At least 20 minutes before baking, do two things: First, position one rack in the upper third and another rack in the lower third of the oven and preheat it to 325°F/165°C/gas 3; second, prepare the boiling water for dipping.

Bring the water to a gentle simmer in a large pot. Just before dipping the pretzels, use a pizza wheel or sharp knife to cut each dough rope into four segments about 5 in/12 cm long. Working in four batches,

continued

use a large skimmer to drop the pretzels gently into the water. Leave them in the water for about 20 seconds, carefully turning them once after 10 seconds. Remove the pretzels from the water, drain, and return them to the baking sheets, spacing them out at least ½ in/12 mm apart. If the twists unwind, simply retwist them. Repeat with the remaining pretzels. Brush the tops of the pretzels with a light coating of the egg wash and sprinkle them with coarse salt.

Bake the pretzels for 20 minutes, and then rotate the pans from front to back and top to bottom. Continue baking until the pretzels are deeply browned, about 17 to 25 minutes more. Remove the baking sheets from the oven and allow the pretzels to cool to room temperature. Once cooled, test a pretzel for doneness by breaking it in half. If the center is still a little chewy, reduce the oven temperature to 300°F/150°C/gas 2 and return the pretzels to the oven to finish hardening to a crisp. This could take anywhere from 10 to 20 minutes more. (Note that if you have some thicker pretzels and some thinner, the thinner ones may be done, while the thicker ones need a little more baking.) Test a pretzel after about 10 minutes, and in 5-minute increments after that. When they are hard, transfer the pretzels to a cooling rack. Once they are completely cooled, store them in an airtight container for up to 2 weeks.

BUTTERY PRETZEL CRACKERS

These buttery crisps are "pretzelized"—sprayed with an alkaline solution to give them that dark color and authentic pretzel flavor. You will need to pick up a plastic spray bottle in order to make this recipe. Store any remaining solution at room temperature in the spray bottle with the nozzle closed, as it will keep indefinitely. (Make sure the bottle can be used to safely store household cleaning products, in which case it will be fine for a lye solution.) Serve these with a cheese plate or a savory dip.

DOUGH

2 cups/255 g unbleached all-purpose flour, plus more for dusting

1 tbsp firmly packed light brown sugar

1 tsp fine sea salt, such as *fleur de sel* or *sel gris*

4 tbsp/55 g cold unsalted butter, cubed

¼ cup plus 3 tbsp/105 ml cold water

ALKALINE SOLUTION

1 cup/240 ml water

1 tsp food-grade lye (see page 20) or 2 tsp baked baking soda (see page 21)

Coarse salt for topping

makes 24 crackers

Whisk together the flour, brown sugar, and fine sea salt in a medium bowl. Use your fingertips to rub the butter into the flour mixture, breaking it up into tiny flour-coated pieces about the size of grains of rice. Add the water and stir with a rubber spatula to form a shaggy mass. Turn the dough out onto an unfloured work surface and knead it 8 to 10 times, just until all of the flour is incorporated. The dough should be slightly tacky but not sticky. If it is sticky, add a little more flour, about 1 tbsp at a time. (If the dough is too dry to come together, add more water, 1 tsp at a time. You are trying to prevent the butter from melting from the warmth of your hands, so the dough will not be a smooth, homogenous mass; rather, specks of butter should be visible.) Cut the dough into two equal portions and form each portion into a disk. Wrap each disk of dough in plastic wrap and refrigerate it for 1 hour.

Before preparing the alkaline solution, read Dipping Pretzels in an Alkaline Solution on page 20.

To prepare the alkaline solution: Pour the 1 cup/240 ml of water into a medium nonreactive bowl. Choose a bowl that is tall enough so that the water comes up no more than 2 in/5 cm from the rim. (Stainless-steel or ceramic bowls are the best choice here; avoid nonstick and

continued

metal surfaces, such as aluminum and copper, which will react with the lye.) Wearing rubber gloves, add the lye or baked baking soda and stir with a metal spoon until it is dissolved. Working in a sink, use a funnel to pour the solution into a spray bottle. Wipe down the sides of the bottle with a wet, soapy sponge or paper towels.

Position one rack in the upper third and another rack in the lower third of the oven and preheat it to 400°F/200°C/gas 6 about 20 minutes before baking. Line two 12-by-17-in/30.5-by-43-cm rimmed baking sheets with parchment paper; set aside.

Lightly dust your work surface and a rolling pin with flour. Working with one disk of dough at a time, roll out the dough into a 10-by-16-in/ 25-by-40.5-cm rectangle, gently pulling and stretching with your hands to form straight edges and sharp corners. Sprinkle the dough with more flour as needed to prevent sticking. Brush any excess flour off the bottom and top of the dough. With the spray bottle set to the finest mist, spray one of the parchment paper–lined baking sheets with the alkaline solution, making sure that the entire surface is covered with a fine coating. Roll the dough up loosely on the rolling pin, and unroll it onto the baking sheet. Trim the edges and cut the dough into twelve rectangular crackers using a pizza cutter or fluted pastry wheel. Spray the tops of the crackers with an even, thorough coating of the alkaline solution. Any areas that are not wet with the solution will not be "pretzelized." Sprinkle the crackers with coarse salt. Repeat this process with the other disk of dough and bake immediately.

Bake the crackers until they are brown and crisp, 12 to 15 minutes, rotating the pans from front to back and top to bottom after 5 minutes of baking, and again after 10 minutes. The crackers may look almost marbled, with some darker spots and some lighter ones from where the alkaline solution was most concentrated. (This just adds to their rustic charm.) Transfer the crackers to a wire rack to cool to room temperature before serving. The crackers will keep at room temperature in an airtight container for up to 2 weeks.

TARALLI

Part cracker, part bread, taralli are little Italian pretzel rings common in the southern part of the boot. They can be either sweet or savory, with a crunchy exterior that gives way to a slight chewiness in the center. I took these savory, fennel seed–studded taralli to a wine party, as the Italians would do, and my friends agreed that they are the ideal snack to accompany a crisp glass of rosé on a spring evening.

2 tsp active dry yeast

½ cup/120 ml warm water (between 100 and 115°F/38 and 45°C)

1 tsp sugar

3½ cups/440 g unbleached all-purpose flour

½ cup/120 ml dry white wine

¼ cup/60 ml extra-virgin olive oil, plus more for greasing the bowl

2 tsp fine sea salt, such as *fleur de sel* or *sel gris*

1½ tbsp fennel seeds, lightly crushed in a mortar and pestle or spice grinder

½ tsp coarsely ground pepper

4 qt/3.8 L water

2 tbsp fine sea salt, such as *fleur de sel* or *sel gris*

1 egg yolk beaten with 1 tbsp water

makes 48

Sprinkle the yeast over the warm water in the bowl of a stand mixer or in a large bowl. Add the sugar, stirring until it is dissolved. Allow the yeast to bloom until it is foamy, 5 to 7 minutes. Add the flour, wine, olive oil, salt, fennel seeds, and pepper to the yeast mixture and stir to form a shaggy mass. Attach the bowl and the dough hook to the stand mixer and begin kneading on medium-low speed. After about 1 minute the dough will form a smooth ball. The dough should be quite firm and may be slightly tacky, but not sticky. (If it is sticky, add a little more flour, about 1 tbsp at a time, and knead it in until the dough is smooth. If the dough is too dry to come together, add more water, 1 tsp at a time.) Continue kneading the dough on medium speed until it is elastic, 5 to 7 minutes. Alternatively, turn the shaggy dough out onto an unfloured work surface and knead it by hand.

Choose a bowl that will be large enough to contain the dough after it has doubled in size, and grease it lightly with olive oil. Transfer the dough to the greased bowl and cover the bowl tightly with plastic wrap. Set the dough aside at room temperature (in a warm spot) to rise until it has doubled in size, about 1½ hours.

Line two 12-by-17-in/30.5-by-43-cm rimmed baking sheets with parchment paper; set aside.

continued

Turn the dough out onto an unfloured work surface and press it down to deflate. Cut it into six equal portions, and divide each portion into eight small chunks of dough. Work with one chunk of dough at a time and keep the rest covered with a damp, clean kitchen towel. Pat a chunk of dough down with your fingertips, and then roll it to form a little cylinder. Roll out the cylinder into a rope that is 12 in/30.5 cm long, working from the center of the dough out to the ends and applying gentle pressure to taper them slightly. Form the rope into a ring by overlapping the dough about ¼ in/6 mm from the ends and gently pinching them together. Place the *taralle* on one of the prepared baking sheets and cover it with a damp towel. Repeat this process with the remaining dough, arranging the *taralli* on a baking sheet at least ¼ in/6 mm apart and covering them with a damp towel. When the first baking sheet is filled with twenty-four *taralli*, transfer it to the refrigerator while you shape the remaining dough to prevent the first batch from overproofing.

When all the *taralli* are shaped, let them rise, covered, at warm room temperature until they have increased in size by about half, 15 to 20 minutes. (The *taralli* can be refrigerated at this point, covered tightly with plastic wrap, for up to 8 hours before dipping and baking them.)

At least 20 minutes before baking, do two things: First, position one rack in the upper third and another rack in the lower third of the oven and preheat it to 325°F/165°C/gas 3; second, prepare the boiling water for dipping.

Bring the water to a gentle simmer in a large pot. Working in eight batches, use a large skimmer to gently drop the *taralli* in the water. Leave them for about 20 seconds, carefully turning once after 10 seconds. Remove the *taralli* from the water, drain, and return them to the baking sheets, spacing them out at least ½ in/12 mm apart. If the ends come detached, simply pinch them back together. Repeat with the remaining dough. Brush the *taralli* with the egg wash just to lightly coat the tops.

Bake the *taralli* until they are light golden brown and crisp, 35 to 40 minutes, rotating the pans from front to back and top to bottom halfway through the baking time. To test for doneness, remove one from the oven and break it in half. If the center is still a little chewy, continue baking. If the color is beginning to darken but the *taralli* are not done inside, remove the trays from the oven and allow them to cool to room temperature while you reduce the oven temperature to 300°F/150°C/gas 2. Return the *taralli* to the oven to finish hardening. Test one after about 10 minutes, and in 5-minute increments after that. Transfer the *taralli* to a cooling rack. They are best eaten the day they are made. Store any remaining *taralli* for a few days in an airtight container. They will become a little soft, so crisp them in a 325°F/165°C/gas 3 oven for a few minutes.

MUSTARD AIOLI

¼ cup/60 ml Spicy Whole-Grain Pub Mustard (page 110) or the mustard of your choice

2 egg yolks

2 garlic cloves, grated on a Microplane or finely minced

2½ tsp fresh lemon juice

1 tsp fine sea salt, such as *fleur de sel* or *sel gris*

½ cup/120 ml canola oil

2 tbsp beer (any style) or water

Peanut or canola oil for deep-frying

1 lb/455 g calamari, whole tubes and tentacles (cleaned by your fishmonger)

1 cup/140 g Pretzel Dust (page 105)

2 tsp fine sea salt, such as *fleur de sel* or *sel gris*, plus more to taste

½ tsp piment d'Espelette (see Cook's Note) or hot paprika

1 cup/240 ml buttermilk

1 lemon wedge

serves 6

PRETZEL-DUSTED CALAMARI
WITH MUSTARD AIOLI

This recipe is inspired by a dish of the same name that has garnered a cult following at Manhattan's ABC Kitchen. Chef Dan Kluger picks up dozens of sourdough hard pretzels from Martin's Pretzels stand at the Union Square Greenmarket and grinds them to a fine powder to bread his crispy fried calamari. (Martin's handmade hard pretzels are an excellent alternative to homemade ones: see Resources, page 124.) If you fear the tedious task of cleaning squid, rest assured that most American fish markets sell them cleaned. That is what I recommend using here. Be sure to fry the calamari in a deep pot to contain any spattering.

To make the Mustard Aioli: Process the mustard, egg yolks, garlic, lemon juice, and salt in a food processor to combine. With the motor running, add the oil in a slow stream through the feed tube. Once the mixture begins to thicken and emulsify into mayonnaise, you can finish adding the oil in a heavier stream. Add the beer and process to combine. Taste and adjust the seasoning. Alternatively, you can make the aioli by hand in a medium bowl, whisking the egg and lemon mixture constantly as you slowly drizzle in the oil. Cover and refrigerate until serving. (You can make the aioli up to 2 days in advance.)

Pour 2 in/5 cm of oil into a large, heavy pot that is at least 5 in/12 cm deep. (Or use an electric deep-fryer, following the manufacturer's instructions for heating the oil.) Heat the oil over medium-high until the temperature registers 375°F/190°C on a deep-fat thermometer, or until a pretzel crumb dropped in the oil sizzles, browns, and then stops sizzling within 30 seconds. Adjust the heat to maintain the temperature. Place a paper towel–lined rimmed baking sheet near the stove top.

While the oil heats, rinse the calamari in a colander under cold running water; drain well. Cut the tubes into ¾-in/2-cm rings.

Put the Pretzel Dust in a large bowl and stir in salt and piment d'Espelette. Pour the buttermilk into another large bowl. Toss the calamari rings and tentacles in the Pretzel Dust to coat each piece evenly. Dump the bowl of calamari and pretzel dust into a colander set over another bowl, and shake to remove the excess pretzel dust. Next, dip the coated calamari in the buttermilk, and then drain it well. Put the calamari back in the bowl with the pretzel dust and toss to coat evenly. Return to the colander and shake out the excess pretzel dust.

When the oil is hot, grab a small handful of the breaded calamari, and carefully drop them into the hot oil using a wire-mesh skimmer. Stand back to avoid any spatter. Fry until the breading is crispy and dark blonde in color, 45 seconds to 1 minute. Remove the calamari from the oil, draining off the excess into the pot, and transfer them to the paper towel–lined baking sheet. Immediately sprinkle them with salt. Allow the oil to return to 375°F/190°C before frying the next batch. Repeat until all of the calamari are fried. Squeeze the lemon over the calamari and serve immediately with the Mustard Aioli for dipping.

COOK'S NOTE

Piment d'Espelette is a fragrant, mildly spicy chile powder that hails from the town of Espelette in the Basque region of France. It can be found at specialty food stores, spice shops, or online. A suitable alternative is hot paprika. Cayenne is significantly spicier, but go for it if heat is your thing.

PRETZEL SCHNITZEL

Four 4-oz/115-g veal cutlets

½ cup/60 g unbleached all-purpose flour

2 large eggs, beaten

1 cup/160 g Pretzel Crumbs (page 105)

Fine sea salt, such as *fleur de sel* or *sel gris*

Freshly ground pepper

Peanut or canola oil for panfrying

4 tbsp/55 g unsalted butter, sliced into pats

4 cups/60 g loosely packed baby arugula

Extra-virgin olive oil for drizzling

1 lemon

serves 4

Austria's national dish is so much cooler with a pretzel coating instead of plain ol' bread crumbs. Wiener schnitzel is a breaded and fried veal cutlet, which has been pounded thin with a meat mallet. Pork cutlets, or boneless loin chops, can be substituted for the veal. Schnitzel is traditionally served with a lemon wedge and potatoes, but I like to lighten it up with a bright baby arugula salad. Or you could bake off a batch of Philadelphia-style soft pretzels (Traditional Soft Pretzels, page 26, made in the Philadelphia-style shape, page 31) and make yourself a "schnitzelwich" with a little mayonnaise and a smear of Tomato-Basil Jam (page 117).

Lay a veal cutlet between two large sheets of plastic wrap, and use a meat mallet or rolling pin to pound the meat to an even ¼-in/6-mm thickness. Transfer it to a baking sheet and repeat with the remaining cutlets.

Set up a three-step breading station: Put the flour, eggs, and Pretzel Crumbs in three separate shallow dishes that are wide enough to hold a cutlet. Stir a pinch of salt into both the flour and the eggs. Pat the veal cutlets dry with paper towels and season both sides with salt and pepper. Dip a cutlet into the flour, coat both sides, and gently shake off the excess. Coat both sides in the egg mixture, letting the excess drip away, and then dip both sides of the cutlet in the Pretzel Crumbs, patting them on firmly so they adhere to and thoroughly coat the cutlet. Return the cutlet to the baking sheet and repeat this process with the remaining meat. Let the cutlets stand at room temperature while you heat the frying oil.

Preheat the oven to 200°F/95°C. Set a cooling rack over a baking sheet and place it near the stove top.

Pour about ¼ in/6 mm of oil into a large, heavy skillet, such as cast iron. Heat the oil until a pretzel crumb dropped into it sizzles, browns, and then stops sizzling within 30 seconds. Add the butter. When it is melted, add two cutlets to the hot fat and cook, turning once, until both sides are crisp and deep golden brown, 2 to 3 minutes per side. Use a large spatula to turn the cutlets rather than tongs or a meat fork, which will hack up the breading. Transfer the cooked cutlets to the cooling rack and put them in the oven to keep warm. Add the other two cutlets to the pan and fry in the same manner, transferring them to the oven to keep warm.

Put the arugula in a large bowl. Drizzle with enough olive oil to lightly coat the leaves. Cut the lemon in half lengthwise and juice a half over the arugula. Season with salt and pepper and toss.

Cut the other half of the lemon into four wedges. Put a schnitzel on each of four warmed plates. Top with a portion of the arugula and serve immediately with a wedge of lemon.

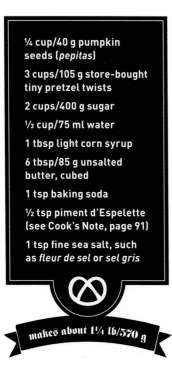

PRETZEL BRITTLE
WITH PEPITAS AND PIMENT D'ESPELETTE

Around the holidays, friends and neighbors would drop off peanut brittle packed into decorative tins at the doorstep of my child-hood home in Columbus, Nebraska. I recall the cloyingly sweet, tooth-defying candy fondly—the stomachaches after eating far too much, not so fondly. This is a grown-up version, with subtle spiciness, saltiness, and soft crunch from the pretzels and pump-kin seeds. It has become my own holiday calling card. I drop it at my friends' doorsteps in vintage tins that I find at thrift stores throughout the year. The leftover bits from breaking the slabs of brittle into shards, I swirl into Pretzel Ice Cream (page 104) and keep for myself.

Toast the pumpkin seeds over medium heat in a dry small sauté pan or skillet until lightly browned and puffed, 5 to 7 minutes. Transfer the seeds to a medium bowl and set aside.

Put the pretzels into a resealable plastic bag and crush them with a rolling pin into ½-in/12-mm pieces. (Or pulse the pretzels in a food processor, if you prefer.) Over a wastebasket, dump the pretzel pieces into a colander and shake it to discard the pretzel dust. Pour the pretzels into the bowl with the pumpkin seeds and set the bowl near the stove top. Line a 12-by-17-in/30.5-by-43-cm rimmed baking sheet with parchment or waxed paper; set aside.

Using a heat-proof silicone spatula or wooden spoon, stir together the sugar, water, and corn syrup in a 2-qt/2-L heavy saucepan over medium heat and cook, stirring, until the sugar dissolves and the liquid is clear, about 10 minutes. Increase the heat to high and stop stirring. Boil the sugar mixture until it turns deep amber, swirling the pan from time to time so the sugar cooks evenly and wiping

continued

down any crystallized sugar on the sides of the pan with a wet pastry brush, 5 to 7 minutes. (Watch carefully because once the caramelized sugar begins to brown, the color darkens quickly and the sugar burns easily.) Test the color by dipping a clean metal spoon into the mixture and dripping a few drops of the caramel on a white plate. Immediately remove the pan from the heat and stir in the butter and baking soda. The mixture will bubble and may spatter, so it is wise to wear an oven mitt on the hand holding the pan. Add the pretzels and pumpkin seeds, the piment d'Espelette, and salt. Return the pan to medium heat and stir to combine the ingredients into a homogenous mixture, about 30 seconds. Quickly pour the hot mixture onto the prepared baking sheet and spread it out to a thin, even layer. Allow the brittle to cool completely into a hard slab, about 20 minutes, and then break it into large shards. It will keep for up to 2 weeks at room temperature in an airtight container.

CARAMEL-CHOCOLATE-PECAN PRETZEL WANDS

Nonstick cooking spray for the foil or waxed paper

TOASTED PECANS

1¼ cups/175 g chopped pecans

CARAMEL

1 cup/200 g sugar

¾ cup/180 ml heavy (whipping) cream

¼ cup/60 ml light corn syrup

2 tbsp unsalted butter, cubed

⅛ tsp fine sea salt, such as *fleur de sel* or *sel gris*

½ tsp pure vanilla extract

12 Hard Pretzel Rods (page 79) or store-bought pretzel rods, such as Snyder's of Hanover

8 oz/225 g bittersweet chocolate, finely chopped

makes 12

For the pretzel lover, this is the ultimate chocolate candy bar, and it even comes with its own handle. Cover your homemade pretzel rods in chewy caramel, melted dark chocolate, and crunchy toasted pecans for a fun food gift. This recipe is adapted from a similar one by my friend and mentor, Diane Morgan. For her book The Christmas Table *she created Chocolate-and-Caramel-Dipped Pretzel Logs to give as holiday treats in cellophane bags tied with bright ribbons. I think that is a festive idea for my pecan-coated pretzel wands, too.*

Lay out a large sheet of waxed paper or aluminum foil and spray it with nonstick cooking spray; you'll use this to collect the dipped pretzels.

To make the Toasted Pecans: Preheat the oven to 350°F/180°C/gas 4. Spread out the pecans in a single layer on a small rimmed baking sheet and toast, stirring once, until fragrant and lightly browned, 6 to 8 minutes. Remove the pecans from the oven and set aside.

To make the Caramel: Bring the sugar, cream, corn syrup, butter, and salt to a boil in a small heavy saucepan over medium-high heat, and cook, stirring constantly with a heat-proof silicone spatula or a wooden spoon, until the sugar is dissolved. Attach a candy thermometer to the side of the pot and continue to boil the mixture until it registers 257°F/125°C, gently stirring, 5 to 7 minutes. Wearing an oven mitt, immediately remove the pan from heat and stir in the vanilla.

One at a time, dip about two-thirds of each pretzel in the caramel, using the spatula to smooth it out and remove the excess. Place the pretzel rods on the waxed paper and allow the caramel to set, about 30 minutes. (If there is leftover caramel, pour it into a small

continued

dish coated with nonstick spray and sprinkle it with a little sea salt. When it is set, cut the caramels into bite-size pieces and wrap them in waxed paper for a bonus treat.)

Have ready a fresh sheet of waxed paper or foil and the chopped pecans nearby. (Do not spray the paper with nonstick spray.) Pour 2 in/5 cm of water into the bottom of a double boiler or a small saucepan. Bring to a boil over high heat. Put three-quarters of the chocolate in the top of the double boiler or into a stainless-steel bowl that will fit inside the saucepan without touching the water. Turn off the heat and set the chocolate over the pot with the water, allowing the steam to melt it slowly, and stirring with a clean, dry spatula. Remove the melted chocolate from the heat and stir in the remaining chocolate. Continue to stir until all the chocolate is melted. If you have one, use an instant-read thermometer to check the temperature of the chocolate. It will stay glossy without any white streaking if the temperature is between 86 and 90°F/30 and 32°C when the pretzels are dipped.

Dip one caramel-covered pretzel at a time, coating the caramel with chocolate and allowing the excess to drip back into the pan. Use a clean spatula to smooth out the melted chocolate over the caramel. Roll the chocolate-coated pretzels in the pecans to collect an even coating. Place the pretzels on the waxed paper or foil coated with cooking spray and allow the chocolate to dry, 1 to 1½ hours. The pretzels will release from the paper once dry. The dipped pretzels keep for up to 1 week. Store them at room temperature in a flat, airtight container between sheets of waxed paper so they are not touching.

3 Pennsylvania Dutch Hard Pretzels (page 76) or store-bought sourdough hard pretzels, such as Martin's Pretzels (see Resources, page 124)

1 cup/250 g crunchy peanut butter

1 cup/200 g firmly packed light brown sugar

1 large egg, beaten

1 tsp baking soda

½ tsp pure vanilla extract

½ tsp fine sea salt, such as *fleur de sel* or *sel gris*

¾ cup/130 g semisweet chocolate chips

Coarse salt for topping

makes 24 cookies

TRIPLE-THREAT COOKIES

Hard pretzel bits, crunchy peanut butter, and chocolate chips make for the ultimate quick-mix cookies—no flour needed. Dip them, warm from the oven, in a stubby glass of cold milk.

Position one rack in the upper third and another rack in the lower third of the oven and preheat it to 350°F/180°C/gas 4. Have ready two ungreased 12-by-17-in/30.5-by-43-cm baking sheets.

Put the pretzels into a resealable plastic bag and crush them with a rolling pin into ½-in/12-mm pieces. (Or pulse the pretzels in a food processor, if you prefer.)

Mix together the peanut butter, brown sugar, egg, baking soda, vanilla, and fine sea salt in a large bowl until homogenous. Mix in the chocolate chips and pretzels until just blended. Form into 1½-in/4-cm balls by packing the pretzel pieces and chocolate chips together with the peanut butter dough, taking care to distribute the chunks evenly. (It's a greasy job, but somebody's got to do it.) Space the cookies 2 in/5 cm apart on the baking sheets and lightly smash them down. Sprinkle each cookie with a little coarse salt.

Bake the cookies until they are puffy and lightly browned on top, 10 to 12 minutes. Rotate the pans from front to back and top to bottom after 5 minutes of baking. Allow the cookies to cool and set on the baking sheets for at least 5 minutes before enjoying. The cookies are best eaten within an hour of baking and still warm from the oven. When they are completely cool, they can be stored in an airtight container for up to 3 days. They harden after a few hours out of the oven, so rewarm the cookies in a 350°F/180°C/gas 4 oven for a few minutes to soften them back up.

CRUST

4 cups/140 g store-bought tiny pretzel twists

1⁄... plus 3 tbsp/155 g unsalted butter, melted

¼ cup/50 g firmly packed light brown sugar

1½ cups/360 ml cold heavy (whipping) cream

½ cup plus 2 tbsp/125 g granulated sugar

2 tsp pure vanilla extract

One 8-oz/225-g package cream cheese

¾ cup/180 ml water

One 3-oz/85-g package strawberry gelatin

About 2 quarts/910 g large fresh strawberries, tops trimmed

serves 10 to 12

RETRO STRAWBERRIES-AND-CREAM PRETZEL TART

When I was growing up in Nebraska in the 1980s, my mom was the queen of what are now considered retro foods from that era. I have fond memories of her pretzel-crusted strawberry Jell-O and cream cheese "salad." Of course, now that I'm a food snob—or food elitist, as my dad would say—I have to give it a slightly more sophisticated rendering. A springform pan is pinch-hitting for the glass Pyrex dish, transforming the salad into a tart. The sides of the pan are removed to reveal the pretty layers. It can be made in a 9-in/23-cm deep-dish pie pan instead, but then I guess it becomes just that, a pie. Salad, tart, pie—whatever you want to call it, this throwback is worth revisiting.

Preheat the oven to 350°F/180°C/gas 4.

To make the Crust: Put the pretzels into a resealable plastic bag and crush them with a rolling pin into pieces that are no larger than ¼ in/6 mm. (Or pulse the pretzels in a food processor, if you prefer.) Pour the crushed pretzels and their crumbs into a medium bowl and stir in the butter and brown sugar. Press the crust mixture into the bottom of a 9-in/23-cm springform pan, covering the bottom of the pan evenly. Bake the crust until it is lightly toasted, 10 to 12 minutes. It will be soft and puffy when you first remove it from the oven, but will harden as it cools. Set the crust aside to cool completely.

Put the bowl of a stand mixer and the whip attachment in the freezer for 10 minutes.

Attach the bowl and the whisk attachment to the mixer, and pour in the cream. Begin whipping the cream on medium speed. When

continued

it starts to thicken, pour in 2 tbsp of the granulated sugar and the vanilla. Whip the cream mixture on medium speed until soft peaks form. (When you dip a spoon into the whipped cream and pull it out, the cream should form a peak that curls back onto itself.) Set aside 1½ cups/360 ml of the whipped cream in a small bowl. Transfer the remaining whipped cream to a separate bowl, cover, and refrigerate; you will use it to top the tart later.

Put the remaining ½ cup/100 g of granulated sugar and the cream cheese in the bowl of the stand mixer. Using the paddle attachment, beat the sugar and cream cheese together on medium speed until creamy, about 2 minutes. Remove the bowl from the mixer, and stir the reserved 1½ cups of whipped cream into the cream cheese mixture until it is homogenous. Spread the cream cheese filling evenly over the cooled crust. Be sure to completely cover the crust, spreading the filling to the edges of the pan. Use a damp paper towel to wipe down any specks of filling clinging to the sides of the pan or the edges of the tart will appear messy when the springform is removed. Refrigerate until chilled and set, 30 minutes.

Meanwhile, bring ½ cup/120 ml of the water to a boil over high heat. Put the gelatin powder in a medium heat-proof bowl and pour in the boiling water. Stir until the gelatin is completely dissolved. Stir in the remaining ¼ cup/60 ml of cold water. Allow the gelatin to cool to room temperature.

While the gelatin cools, arrange the strawberries, cut-side down, over the cream cheese filling to cover the entire top of the tart. Start by lining the edge of the tart with a ring of strawberries and work your way to the center in a target pattern. The tips of the berries should be pointing straight up. Pour the gelatin over the strawberries and cream cheese layer, coating the tops of the strawberries in the gelatin as you pour. Refrigerate, covered, until the gelatin is completely set, at least 1 hour. (The tart can be refrigerated up to 1 day before serving.)

Remove the sides of the pan and transfer the tart (still on the springform base) to a serving platter. Gently rewhisk the reserved whipped cream for 10 to 15 seconds and pile it in the center of the tart, if you wish, or pass at the table. Slice and serve immediately.

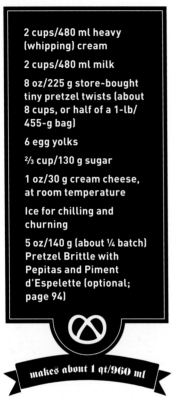

2 cups/480 ml heavy (whipping) cream

2 cups/480 ml milk

8 oz/225 g store-bought tiny pretzel twists (about 8 cups, or half of a 1-lb/ 455-g bag)

6 egg yolks

²⁄₃ cup/130 g sugar

1 oz/30 g cream cheese, at room temperature

Ice for chilling and churning

5 oz/140 g (about ¼ batch) Pretzel Brittle with Pepitas and Piment d'Espelette (optional; page 94)

makes about 1 qt/960 ml

PRETZEL ICE CREAM

Flecked by crunchy bits of pretzel brittle, this is sure to be the next hot flavor on the ice-cream scene. The unusual salty, bread-tinged custard is enhanced by a surprisingly buttery richness. A hunk of cream cheese adds extra smoothness and a little tang. For those who prefer their ice cream velvety and unadulterated, the brittle is an optional addition.

Bring the cream and milk to a simmer over medium-high heat in a large, heavy saucepan, stirring occasionally. Put the pretzels in a large heat-proof bowl; set aside.

Whisk together the egg yolks, sugar, and cream cheese in a medium heat-proof bowl to form a thick paste. Off the heat, slowly whisk about 1 cup/240 ml of the hot cream mixture into the egg mixture to temper the yolks. Whisk the tempered eggs into the pot with the cream mixture and continue to cook the custard over medium heat, gently stirring, until it thickens just enough to coat the back of a spoon, 5 to 8 minutes.

Remove the custard from the heat and pour it into the bowl with the pretzels. Put the bowl into a larger bowl filled with ice water and stir until the custard has cooled to room temperature. Strain the custard through a fine-mesh strainer into another container and discard the soggy pretzels. Cover the custard and refrigerate until completely chilled, at least 4 hours and up to 24 hours, before churning.

If you are adding the pretzel brittle, put it into a resealable plastic bag and smack it with a rolling pin to break it into pea-size pieces. Dump the contents of the bag into a colander set over a wastebasket and shake it to discard the minuscule crumbs.

When the custard is completely chilled and thickened, stir in the brittle. Churn the custard in an ice-cream maker according to the manufacturer's instructions. Put the ice cream in the freezer until it is firm enough to scoop, about 4 hours. The ice cream will keep in the freezer for about 1 week.

PRETZEL BITS AND PIECES

CROUTONS

Turn two-day-old or stale soft pretzels into crispy little nuggets to top salads and soups. Croutons can be made from pretzels of any shape. Cut them into bite-size cubes and toss them with a light coating of good-quality extra-virgin olive oil and a sprinkle of minced fresh rosemary, fine sea salt, and freshly ground pepper. Spread them out on a rimmed baking sheet and bake in a 400°F/200°C/gas 6 oven until they are browned around the edges and hard throughout, 7 to 12 minutes, stirring once. Cool and store them in an airtight container at room temperature for up to 4 days.

CROSTINI

Tiny pretzel toasts make the ideal base for savory spreads and cute little canapés. Make crostini from leftover soft pretzels in the shape of torpedo rolls (page 33), or twists or braided rings (page 34). Cut the pretzel breads into ¼-in-/8-mm-thick slices. Halve a large garlic clove and rub both sides of the breads with the cut side of the garlic. (Discard the garlic or use it in another recipe.) Arrange the breads on a rimmed baking sheet. Brush them lightly with good-quality extra-virgin olive oil and sprinkle them with fine sea salt. Bake in a 400°F/200°C/gas 6 oven until they are toasty and browned around the edges, 10 to 12 minutes, turning them over halfway through the baking time. Cool and store them in an airtight container at room temperature for up to 2 days.

PRETZEL CRUMBS

Use pretzel crumbs in place of conventional bread crumbs to coat anything you plan to bread and fry or top and bake. To make them, spread out cubed soft pretzels on a rimmed baking sheet and toast them in a 325°F/165°C/gas 3 oven until they are completely dried out, about 7 to 12 minutes, depending on how stale they are to begin with. Grind the dehydrated pretzels in a food processor to the desired coarseness. Keep the crumbs larger for crunchier, panko-style bread crumbs, or finer for a crispier coating. You can also make even crunchier crumbs by grinding Pennsylvania Dutch Hard Pretzels, whether homemade (page 76) or store-bought. Store the crumbs in an airtight container at room temperature for up to 3 weeks.

PRETZEL DUST

Powdery pretzel dust delivers an ultrafine coating—similar to Wondra flour or rice flour—for dredging fish before pan-searing, or for tossing seafood and vegetables before deep-frying. Use it in the recipe for Pretzel-Dusted Calamari with Mustard Aioli (page 90). To make it, process Pennsylvania Dutch Hard Pretzels (page 76) in a food processor for several minutes until powdery. Dump the powder into a fine-mesh strainer set over a bowl, and discard the larger crumbs. The pretzel dust can be stored in an airtight container at room temperature for 3 weeks.

MUSTARDS, DIPS, AND SPREADS

Dipping pretzels is an American custom. In Germany, they are consumed simply with a pat of butter, like other breads. Often they accompany a sausage, and only then would they be served with mustard (the mustard serving as an accoutrement for the sausage, not the pretzel). In America, we like them with mustard, even without a sausage. Grocers' shelves are lined with interesting mustards these days—fruity, herby, sweet, spiced, beer-based, they are all there. So why make your own? Well, first, homemade is more piquant and carries a fresher, truer flavor than anything you'll buy in a jar. Furthermore, since you are perusing this book, you must be a bit of a project-seeking cook, and homemade mustard is a must for your repertoire. Mustard is indeed a project, but a worthwhile one at that. The traditional method takes time—at least two to three weeks for it to reach its peak palatability—but a couple of the mustards in this chapter are same-day preparations, and one rests just overnight. Beyond mustard, there are many other sweet and savory dips and spreads that are worthy of accompanying your homemade pretzels, of both the soft and hard varieties.

2 cups/480 ml apple cider vinegar

1 cup/240 ml water

1 onion, diced

¼ cup plus 2 tbsp /75 g firmly packed dark brown sugar

2 tsp fine sea salt, such as *fleur de sel* or *sel gris*

One 3-in/7.5-cm cinnamon stick

6 whole allspice berries

6 whole cloves

2 tsp ground turmeric

½ cup/100 g yellow mustard seeds

¼ cup/50 g brown mustard seeds

makes about 2 cups/480 ml

SWEET BAVARIAN MUSTARD

*This Old World mustard recipe is an authentic replica of the sweet-style mustard that is served at any **Biergarten** in Bavaria. Prepare it at least a few days, and preferably a week, before you plan to dip your pretzels.*

Combine the vinegar, water, onion, brown sugar, salt, cinnamon stick, allspice, cloves, and turmeric in a medium saucepan. Bring the mixture to a boil over medium-high heat. Allow the liquid to boil rapidly to reduce the volume by half, about 10 minutes.

Put the yellow and brown mustard seeds in a medium heat-proof bowl. Strain the hot vinegar mixture through a fine-mesh strainer into the bowl of mustard seeds. Use a heat-proof silicone spatula to press the onions into the strainer to extract all of the liquid. Push the mustard seeds down to completely submerge them in the liquid, cover, and refrigerate for 24 hours.

Transfer the seeds and liquid to a food processor and process until it forms a smooth paste. Put the mustard in an airtight container and refrigerate for at least a 3 days, and preferably 1 week, before serving to allow its pungency to mellow. After about 2 weeks, the mustard is at its prime. It will keep, refrigerated, for several months. If the mustard becomes too thick as it matures, thin it out by adding a splash of vinegar or water.

4 egg yolks

3 tbsp firmly packed light brown sugar

¼ cup/60 ml Champagne vinegar or white wine vinegar

¼ cup/25 g yellow mustard powder

1½ tsp fine sea salt, such as *fleur de sel* or *sel gris*

⅓ cup/75 ml water

3 tbsp minced fresh sweet herbs, such as tarragon, chives, and dill

makes about 1 cup/240 ml

HERBACEOUS MUSTARD

Here yellow mustard powder is heated and releases its flavor immediately for a speedy pretzel dip. The rich, egg-based sauce delivers a calmer heat than other homemade mustards, but it is still quite spicy. It keeps just a few days in the refrigerator—that is, if there is any left over.

Pour about 1½ in/4 cm of water into a saucepan that is big enough to hold a large stainless-steel bowl, creating a double-boiler, and bring the water to a boil over high heat. Reduce the heat to maintain a low simmer.

In the large stainless-steel bowl, beat the egg yolks with the brown sugar. Whisk in the vinegar, mustard powder, salt, and the water. Set the bowl over the pot of gently simmering water, making sure that the water doesn't touch the bottom of the bowl. Cook the mixture, whisking constantly, until it thickens to the consistency of a loose mustard, 2½ to 3 minutes. (It should be saucy at this point; it will continue to thicken as it cools.) Remove the bowl from the heat and stir in the herbs. Transfer the hot mustard to a glass bowl or jar and refrigerate to cool. The mustard will keep, covered, in the refrigerator for up to 4 days.

SPICY WHOLE-GRAIN PUB MUSTARD

¼ cup/50 g yellow mustard seeds

¼ cup/50 g brown mustard seeds

¾ cup/180 ml German *Doppelbock* beer, such as Ayinger Brewery's Celebrator (see page 13)

¼ cup/60 ml apple cider vinegar

2 tbsp honey

2 tbsp firmly packed dark brown sugar

2 large garlic cloves, smashed

1 bay leaf

2 tsp fine sea salt, such as *fleur de sel* or *sel gris*

⅛ tsp freshly ground pepper

makes about 1⅓ cups/315 ml

With this smokin' hot whole-grain beer mustard to dip your pretzels in, you'll have the pretzel aficionado's holy trinity—beer, mustard, and pretzels—in each bite. Prepare it at least a few days before you plan to dunk so the astringency of the mustard seeds morphs into a spicy heat. The flavor of this mustard is at its best after maturing for at least 3 weeks.

Put the yellow and brown mustard seeds in a nonreactive bowl and pour in ½ cup/120 ml of the beer. Push the mustard seeds down to completely submerge them in the beer, cover, and refrigerate for 24 hours.

Combine the remaining ¼ cup/60 ml of beer, the vinegar, honey, brown sugar, garlic, bay leaf, salt, and pepper in a small saucepan. Bring the mixture to a boil over medium-high heat, stirring to dissolve the honey and sugar. Boil for 1 minute, and then immediately remove the pan from the heat and cool the liquid to room temperature.

Discard the garlic and bay leaf and pour the liquid into a blender. Add the plumped mustard seeds and blend until about half the seeds are ground, the rest remain whole, and the mustard is thickened to the desired consistency. Put the mustard in an airtight container and refrigerate for at least 3 days, and preferably 1 week, before serving to allow its pungency to mellow. After about 3 weeks, the mustard will be at its prime. It will keep, refrigerated, for several months. If the mustard becomes too thick as it ages, thin it out by stirring in a splash of beer or vinegar.

1 tbsp fennel seeds

1 tbsp yellow mustard
seeds

1½ tsp caraway seeds

4 egg yolks

2 tbsp firmly packed light
brown sugar

⅓ cup/75 ml malt vinegar

¼ cup/60 ml aquavit

3 tbsp yellow mustard
powder

1 tsp fine sea salt, such
as *fleur de sel* or *sel gris*

Dash of Worcestershire
sauce

makes about 1 cup/240 ml

SPICED AQUAVIT MUSTARD

Chef Ben Bettinger created the ideal bar snack for Beaker and Flask, a restaurant in Portland, Oregon: three crusty pretzel sticks, accompanied by a small glass of beer and this intoxicating mustard sauce. Aromatic fennel and caraway seeds complement the flavors of aquavit, a spice-infused Scandinavian liquor. The best part is that this mustard can be made and served the same day; no maturation time is needed.

Pour about 1½ in/4 cm of water into a saucepan that is big enough to hold a large stainless-steel bowl, creating a double-boiler, and bring the water to a boil over high heat. Reduce the heat to maintain the water at a low simmer.

Meanwhile, place a dry small, heavy frying pan over medium-high heat. Add the fennel seeds, mustard seeds, and caraway seeds and toast, swirling the pan constantly until the seeds are fragrant and lightly browned, about 1 minute. Transfer the seeds to a mortar and pestle or a spice grinder and grind to a fine powder.

In the large stainless-steel bowl, beat the egg yolks with the brown sugar. Whisk in the ground spice mixture, vinegar, aquavit, mustard powder, salt, and Worcestershire sauce. Set the bowl over the pot of gently simmering water, making sure that the water does not touch the bottom of the bowl. Cook the mixture, whisking gently but constantly, until it thickens to a saucy consistency, about 3 minutes. (Note that the mustard will continue to thicken as it cools.) Transfer the hot mustard to a glass bowl or jar, cover, and refrigerate to cool. The mustard is ready to eat immediately, and it will keep, refrigerated, for up to 4 days.

½ cup/100 g yellow
mustard seeds

½ cup/120 ml dry
Riesling wine

⅔ cup/165 g good-quality
apricot jam

2 tsp fine sea salt, such
as *fleur de sel* or *sel gris*

makes about 1½ cups/360 ml

APRICOT-RIESLING MUSTARD

*An overnight soak in a Riesling bath, followed by a healthy dose of
chunky apricot jam, mellow this mustard to palatable pungency.
The heat is balanced with sweet nectar notes after just a few hours
of aging. You'll get bonus points if you use your own homemade
apricot jam; otherwise, be sure to choose a good-quality jar at the
market. I find this to be an especially enjoyable hard pretzel accoutrement. Similar to a mostarda, it also serves a thick slice of pork
terrine quite well.*

Put the mustard seeds in a small nonreactive bowl and pour in the
Riesling. Push the seeds down to completely submerge them in
the wine. Cover and refrigerate overnight, or until the seeds have
absorbed most of the wine.

Transfer the plumped mustard seeds to a food processor and
process until about half the seeds are ground and the rest remain
whole, scraping down the sides as needed. Return the seeds to the
bowl and stir in the apricot jam and salt. The mustard is ready to
enjoy immediately, but it will keep in the refrigerator for 1 month
or more. Note that the pungency of the mustard will mellow as it
ages. Serve the mustard at room temperature for maximum flavor.

BEER CHEESE FONDUE

1 cup/240 ml pilsner-style beer

1 lb/455 g Gruyère cheese, shredded

1 tbsp cornstarch

2 tsp Sweet Bavarian Mustard (page 108) or store-bought Dijon mustard

Dash of Worcestershire sauce

Pinch of paprika

Fine sea salt, such as *fleur de sel* or *sel gris*

serves 6 to 8

Soft pretzels, sliced German sausages, pickled garden vegetables, and roasted Brussels sprouts can all be dipped in this oozy cheese sauce for one amusing wintertime party. Swiss Alpine-style cheeses are the best choice for fondue, given their earthy, robust flavor and excellent melting quality. Substitute any easy-melting cheese for the Gruyère found in this recipe. Raclette, Emmentaler, Cheddar, Fontina, and Gouda are all delicious choices, and can be blended for a more complex flavor.

Bring the beer to a boil over medium-high heat in a fondue pot or a medium heavy saucepan. Reduce the heat to medium-low so the beer is gently simmering.

Toss the Gruyère with the cornstarch in a medium bowl. Add the cheese mixture to the beer one large handful at a time, stirring the cheese in a figure-eight pattern until completely melted before adding more. Stir in the mustard, Worcestershire sauce, and paprika, and season with salt. Serve immediately. The fondue can be refrigerated, covered, for up to 2 days and then rewarmed over medium-low heat, stirring in a figure-eight pattern, until the cheese is melted and hot.

NACHO CHEESE

1½ tbsp unsalted butter

½ cup/70 g finely diced onion

2 jalapeño peppers, seeded, deribbbed, and minced

1 tbsp cornstarch

1 cup/240 ml whole or 2 percent milk

2 oz/60 g cream cheese, cubed

5 oz/140 g sharp Cheddar cheese, shredded

2 oz/55 g Monterey Jack cheese, shredded

⅓ cup/60 g diced tomato

1 tsp hot sauce, such as Cholula or Tabasco sauce

1 tsp sea salt, such as *fleur de sel* or *sel gris*

¼ tsp sweet paprika

makes 2 cups/480 ml

Though still a guilty pleasure, nacho cheese is so much better when it is homemade. Who knows what is in the processed cheese sauce that is pumped out at sports arenas across America. To get that craveably rich, smooth texture with good-quality cheese and natural ingredients was a challenge. After a few experiments, I found that adding a dollop of cream cheese and a little cornstarch produced that velvety creaminess and the right thickness.

Melt the butter in a medium heavy saucepan over medium heat. Add the onion and jalapeño and cook, stirring occasionally, until they are soft but not browned, 6 to 8 minutes. Add the cornstarch, stirring until it dissolves into a paste. Whisk in the milk and cream cheese and bring the mixture to a low simmer, whisking until the cream cheese is melted. Reduce the heat to low. Add about half of the Cheddar cheese and use a heat-proof silicone spatula or wooden spoon to stir it in a figure-eight pattern. When it is completely melted, add the remaining Cheddar. Once that is melted, add the Monterey Jack and stir until all the cheese has melted, leaving you with a smooth sauce. Stir in the tomato, hot sauce, salt, and paprika. Taste and adjust the seasoning, adding more hot sauce to reach the desired spiciness. Serve immediately or transfer the nacho cheese to a fondue pot or a small slow cooker and keep hot.

Nacho cheese can be made up to 2 days in advance and refrigerated, covered, until served. Reheat the sauce over low heat in a small saucepan, stirring often, until the cheese is melted, saucy, and hot.

TOMATO-BASIL JAM

1½ tbsp extra-virgin olive oil

1 red onion, diced

2½ lb/1.2 kg plum tomatoes

1 large garlic clove, minced

3 tbsp firmly packed light brown sugar

2 tbsp tomato paste

2 tbsp balsamic vinegar

2 tsp fine sea salt, such as *fleur de sel* or *sel gris*

10 basil leaves, thinly sliced

makes about 2 cups/520 g

Summer's most glorious tomatoes make this savory jam a winning pretzel dip. Consider this a welcome replacement for the canned marinara sauce that is served with soft pretzels in shopping mall food courts. Your homemade pretzels deserve much, much better. Use the jam as a sweet and tart spread for your Pretzel Grilled Cheese (page 60), as a sauce on Philadelphia-Style soft pretzels (see page 31) with Pepperoni Pizza topping (see page 35), or as a dip for any pretzel you desire, whether soft or hard.

Heat a medium Dutch oven or another heavy pot over medium-low heat. Add the olive oil and swirl to coat the pot. Add the onion and cook, stirring occasionally, until extremely soft and lightly browned, about 20 minutes.

Meanwhile, cut the tomatoes in half lengthwise. Using the coarsest side of a box grater, grate the tomato flesh into a large bowl by placing the cut side against the grater and grating it down until just the skin remains beneath your palm. Discard the skins and set the grated tomato aside.

Stir the garlic into the pot with the onions and cook until it is aromatic, about 1 minute. Add the brown sugar and tomato paste and cook, stirring often, until the color deepens to rusty red, about 2 minutes. Stir in the grated tomatoes, balsamic vinegar, and salt. Increase the heat to high and bring the mixture to a boil. Reduce the heat to medium-high and cook, stirring occasionally. After 20 to 25 minutes, when the mixture thickens and begins to spatter, reduce the heat to medium. Continue to cook, stirring often, until it is reduced to about a quarter of the original volume and has a jam-like consistency, 35 to 45 minutes more. Remove the tomato jam from the heat and stir in the basil. Taste and adjust the seasoning. Serve the jam hot, or transfer it to a pint-size glass canning jar or another sealable container and refrigerate to cool it. The leftover jam will keep in the refrigerator, covered, for 1 week.

1 cup/225 g unsalted butter, at room temperature

¼ cup plus 2 tbsp/85 g prepared horseradish

¼ cup/15 g minced fresh flat-leaf parsley

½ tsp fine sea salt, such as *fleur de sel* or *sel gris*

makes 1⅓ cups/305 g

HORSERADISH-PARSLEY BUTTER

The contrast of cold butter on a warm pretzel is a thing of beauty. I've heard that in Germany, to eat a pretzel with mustard is like eating a hotdog bun with ketchup and mustard, sans the dog—it simply isn't done unless there is a sausage involved. Germans eat pretzels with butter, like the French eat baguettes. Call this an ode to German tradition.

Beat together the butter, horseradish, parsley, and salt on medium-high speed in the bowl of an electric mixer fitted with the paddle attachment, or with a hand mixer in a medium bowl. Spread out a large sheet of plastic wrap on your work surface, and spoon the butter down the center, lengthwise. Encase the butter in the plastic wrap and roll it into a cylinder, about 1½ in/4 cm in diameter. Wrap it tightly in another piece of plastic wrap and twist and secure the ends with kitchen twine or twisty ties. Refrigerate the butter until chilled, and then slice it into thick pats to serve. (Alternatively, you can pack the butter into a small ramekin.) Use the butter within 3 days, or store it in the freezer, where it will keep for 1 month or more. Defrost to serve.

One 8-oz/225-g package cream cheese, at room temperature

1 tbsp powdered sugar

2½ tsp grated lemon zest

1 tsp pure vanilla extract

Fine sea salt, such as *fleur de sel* or *sel gris*

makes 1 heaping cup/220 g

WHIPPED CREAM CHEESE
WITH LEMON AND VANILLA

Fluffy, rich, and softly sweet, this creamy spread is meant to accompany cinnamon-raisin pretzels (Traditional Soft Pretzels, see page 26, made with Cinnamon-Raisin Pretzel Dough, page 30) at breakfast time.

Beat together the cream cheese, sugar, lemon zest, vanilla, and a pinch of salt in the bowl of an electric mixer fitted with the paddle attachment on medium speed. Or use a hand mixer and a medium bowl. When the mixture is homogenous, increase the speed to medium-high and continue to whip until the cream cheese is light and creamy and has increased in volume by about a quarter. Serve immediately or chill. The spread will keep in the refrigerator, covered, for up to 1 week.

1½ cups/360 ml heavy (whipping) cream

1 vanilla bean

1 cup/200 g sugar

1 tbsp light corn syrup

¼ cup/60 ml water

4 tbsp/55 g cold unsalted butter, cubed

1½ tsp fine sea salt, such as *fleur de sel* or *sel gris*

makes 2 cups/480 ml

SALTED CARAMEL SAUCE

Plunge hard pretzels into this sauce, drizzle it over Pretzel Ice Cream (page 104), melt it over Pretzel Bread Pudding (page 71)— caramel sauce laced with sea salt knows no bounds.

Pour the cream into a small saucepan. Slit the vanilla bean lengthwise down the center and use the back of the knife to scrape out the seeds from one of the halves into the cream; add the empty pod half. (Wrap the other half of the vanilla bean tightly in plastic wrap and reserve it for another use.) Warm the vanilla cream over medium-high heat until it is foamy around the edges, stirring occasionally. Discard the empty vanilla pod half and set the vanilla cream aside.

Using a heat-proof silicone spatula or wooden spoon, combine the sugar, corn syrup, and water in a medium heavy saucepan over medium heat and cook, stirring, until the sugar dissolves and the liquid is clear. Increase the heat to high and stop stirring. Boil the sugar mixture until it turns deep amber, 5 to 7 minutes, swirling the pan from time to time to cook the sugar evenly and using a wet pastry brush to wipe down any crystallized sugar on the sides of the pan. (The sugar burns easily, so watch carefully.) Test the color by dipping a clean metal spoon into the mixture and dripping a few drops of the caramel on a white plate. Immediately remove the pan from the heat and very slowly pour in the warm vanilla cream. The mixture will spatter and bubble violently, almost to the point of overflowing. It is wise to wear an oven mitt on the hand holding the saucepan.

Return the pan to medium heat and whisk to melt any solidified caramel, about 1 minute. Remove the pan from the heat and whisk in the butter and salt. Serve the caramel hot or at room temperature. The caramel will keep in an airtight container in the refrigerator for up to 2 weeks. Allow it to come to room temperature before serving, or reheat in a double boiler over low heat or in the microwave at 50 percent power in 30-second increments until warm.

DARK CHOCOLATE–PEANUT BUTTER DUNK

¾ cup/180 ml heavy (whipping) cream

4½ oz/130 g bittersweet chocolate, finely chopped

¼ cup/80 g creamy peanut butter

2 tsp brandy (optional)

¼ tsp pure vanilla extract

¼ tsp fine sea salt, such as *fleur de sel* or *sel gris*

makes about 1½ cups/360 ml

Nothing marries better than chocolate and peanut butter. Throw some homemade hard pretzels into the mix and you've got a delectable ménage à trois. Essentially a ganache with the decadent addition of creamy peanut butter, this dunk can be served warm or at room temperature. Use a fine-quality dark chocolate, such as Valrhona, for optimal luxuriousness. Be sure to chop the chocolate into small pieces, no larger than peas, so that it melts smoothly in its bath of steamy cream.

Heat the cream in a small saucepan over medium heat, stirring occasionally, until it is just barely simmering. Mix together the chocolate and peanut butter in a medium heat-proof bowl. Pour the hot cream over the chocolate and peanut butter. Let the mixture stand for about 2 minutes to melt the chocolate. Whisk until it is smooth and well combined. Stir in the brandy, if using, the vanilla, and salt. Serve warm or at room temperature.

The sauce will keep in the refrigerator, covered, for up to 1 week. Reheat in a double boiler over low heat or in the microwave at 50 percent power in 30-second increments until warm.

RESOURCES

FLOUR

Bob's Red Mill
www.bobsredmill.com
Rye, spelt, whole-wheat, and gluten-free flours

King Arthur Flour
www.kingarthurflour.com
Bread flour. They also carry high-heat parchment
paper, pretzel salt, and barley malt syrup.

FOOD-GRADE LYE

Amazon
www.amazon.com

Essential Depot
www.essentialdepot.com

HANDMADE PENNSYLVANIA
DUTCH HARD PRETZELS

Hammond Pretzel Bakery
www.hammondpretzels.com

Martin's Pretzels
www.martinspretzels.com

Uncle Jerry's Pretzels
www.unclejerryspretzels.com

SALT

The Great American Spice Co.
www.americanspice.com
Pretzel salt

The Meadow
www.atthemeadow.com
Artisan salt

Spice Barn
www.spicebarn.com
Pretzel salt

INDEX

ACKNOWLEDGMENTS

Five years ago, the idea that I would one day write a cookbook seemed about as realistic as becoming a rock star. But, then I met Diane Morgan. Thank you, Diane, for teaching me everything you know about cookbook writing and encouraging me to pursue my dream.

My sincerest thanks to the following:

The team at Chronicle Books, especially Amy Treadwell for getting excited about pretzels and giving me the opportunity to write about them; managing editors Doug Ogan and Claire Fletcher; production coordinator Tera Killip; designer Alice Chau; marketing manager Peter Perez; publicity manager David Hawk.

Alex Farnum, the mood of your beautiful images is exactly what I hoped for: rich, dark, earthy, and manly—just like pretzels.

My agent, Lisa Ekus, and the team at The Lisa Ekus Group, thank you for helping me with my first book in so many ways. I look forward to many more together.

My girlfriends in the 'hood—Lila Martin, Brenda Crow, and Caroline Ford—who were always willing to share a beer and taste test a pretzel. You have the most discerning palates, and I'm ever so grateful for the advice and support you gave.

Benjamin Bettinger, you've been one of my most important teachers, and your friendship means so much to me.

My BFF, Nicole French Furtaw, for your friendship and support in everything I do, always.

David Reamer—a photo shoot with this guy is always a pleasure. Thank you for making me look good (I know that was a lot of work).

Mark Bitterman, for recommending the perfect pretzel salts.

The enthusiastic pretzel testers: Casey Barber, Katie Burnett, Delia Chiu, Ashley Gartland, Jolene George, Heather Jones, Cristie Mather, Alex Nydahl, and Jo Ostgarden.

The brilliant pretzel bakers that welcomed me into their shops to learn how an authentic pretzel is made: Edgar Loesch of Fressen Bakery in Portland, Oregon; Lina Kulchinsky at Sigmund Pretzel Shop in New York City; and all the folks at the Julius Sturgis Pretzel Bakery in Lititz, Pennsylvania.

Much love to my aunt and uncle, Phil and Jane Rapone, and my cousin, Lauren Clapper, who took me to Pennsylvania Dutch Country in the name of research. What a fun day!

Finally, my family—mom, dad, Allie, and Tom—thank you for being so supportive of me. I love you all very much.